The Knight

Alan Baker

WILEY

John Wiley & Sons, Inc.

Published by John Wiley & Sons, Inc., Hoboken, New Jersey
Published simultaneously in Canada

For general information about our other products and services, please contact our Customer Care Department within the United States at (800) 762-2974, outside the United States at (317) 572-3993 or fax (317) 572-4002.

Wiley also publishes its books in a variety of electronic formats. Some content that appears in print may not be available in electronic books. For more information about Wiley products, visit our web site at www.wiley.com.

Library of Congress Cataloging-in-Publication Data:

Baker, Alan.
The knight / Alan Baker.
p.   cm.
Includes bibliographical references and index.
ISBN 0-471-25135-6
1. Knights and knighthood — Europe — History.
2. Civilization, Medieval.   I. Title.
CR4513.B32   2003
940.1'088'355 — dc21   2002009956

Printed in the United States of America

10 9 8 7 6 5 4 3 2 1

This book is for Zahid Aslam, old friend.

Contents

Introduction

Today, when we think of the knight as a historical figure, we think immediately of courage, loyalty, courtesy, honor, and the violent glories of battle — in
fact, all the archetypal qualities associated with "the knight in
shining armor." Was this really the truth of knighthood?
Were knights really the paragons of virtue many people assume them to be? Who *were* the knights? What were their
lives really like? In this book we will become acquainted
with the life of the knight, with the ways in which he was
groomed for the profession, the methods by which he was
ordained, and the vows he took. We will follow his day-to-
day life as well as his training in preparation for the military
service he undertook for his liege lord, not to mention the
tournaments and jousts in which he would participate on
happier, more peaceful days, as noblemen and fine ladies
watched in awe the demonstration of his many skills. Finally,
we will go into battle with him and meet his foes head-on,
examining their tactics and weapons.

A knight was, fundamentally, a mounted warrior who
fought in the service of his liege lord. In combat, these warriors had a considerable advantage over those fighting on
foot: not only could they charge with great speed and

momentum, they could also crush their enemies beneath the hooves of their horses, pierce them with their lances while remaining beyond the reach of their opponents' weapons, and exit the battle immediately and at a moment's notice, only to return once again for another lightning-fast assault. Thus, during the medieval period, the horse-mounted soldier was the most significant element in an army, and it is no surprise that the root of the French word for knight, *chevalier*, is the word for horse, *cheval*.

Broadly speaking, the age of the mounted warrior lasted throughout the medieval period, a span of some one thousand years, although in this book we will concern ourselves primarily with the period in which he was most active as a military force: roughly from the tenth to the sixteenth centuries. Such is the richness and complexity of the history of knighthood that a book of this length cannot hope to cover it in its entirety; indeed, each of the subjects covered in the chapters you are about to read have themselves inspired numerous books and countless scholarly papers over many decades of research. For this reason I have limited myself to introducing and describing the key elements of knights and knighthood, in the hope that the general reader encountering them for the first time will be sufficiently intrigued to pursue a deeper study of this gruesome yet fascinating period of history.

In each chapter we shall examine a particular aspect of the knight and his life, ranging from the feudal system by which he received his livelihood, to the weapons and armor he used, the castles in which he lived and for which he fought, the food he ate, the chivalric code that dictated his conduct in love and in war, and finally the advances in battlefield technology that eventually made the knight all but obsolete. I have also decided to illustrate the information presented by describing one or more relevant events from the time, thus, I hope, providing the reader with a lasting impression of medieval life. Some of these events are of paramount historical importance, such as the fall of Jerusalem at the end of the eleventh century, described in chapter 6 through the life of Duke Godfrey of Bouillon, who led the armies of Christendom into the Holy City to perpetrate one of the worst massacres of the period, and whom the travel writer and historian Tim Severin rightly calls "the perfect symbol of the Crusade."

Other episodes are in themselves of far less importance in historical terms, and yet provide us with a fascinating insight into the ways in which the knights of the medieval period conducted themselves. The first chapter is devoted to an explanation of the role of the knight in medieval society, including his training and investiture, and also the often deadly dangers to which he was exposed in his quest for glory. We shall also experience the pomp and ceremony that accompanied his funeral. Chapter 2 will describe the social system known as feudalism, which was of enormous importance to the way in which the knight lived his life and earned his living. In this chapter we shall observe a four-day jousting tournament (described at length by Jean Froissart in his *Chronicles*) held at St. Inglevert in northern France between three French knights and a large contingent of English who crossed the Channel to accept their challenge.

The next chapter will describe the essential equipment of the knight: his weapons, armor, and warhorse, each of which had to be of the very highest quality if he was to preserve his life and honor on the bloody battlefields of the Middle Ages.

After pausing briefly to sample the medieval diet (which may include some stomach-churning surprises for the modern reader), we will move on to the complex code of chivalry by which the knight conducted himself. This illustrates very well the extremes of behavior that formed routine aspects of the knight's life and personality; for, while he could treat his enemies with the utmost barbarity (catapulting the severed heads of prisoners over a castle wall was a particular favorite in his arsenal of psychological warfare), he also could be capable of great fairness and gentility, and the practice of "courtly love" is in itself legendary for its emphasis on respect for and admiration of women.

Of course, the knight did not spend his entire life charging into battle, jousting with his fellows, or practicing courtly love; much of his time was spent at rest or seeing to the management of his estates, and here we encounter the other great image associated with the medieval period: the castle. In a sense the castle can be seen as part of the knight's equipment; not only was it his home, it also was the headquarters from which he controlled the lands of his fief. In addition, it was the primary target of his enemies wishing to take what was his, for when a castle fell, all was lost to the owner. Like his other equipment, the castle evolved over the centuries, gradually improving in design and construction. Its defenses were as numerous as the great siege engines designed to defeat them; in fact, sieges were far more common than battles, and for this reason we shall take some time to examine the methods by which they were conducted, in chapter 5.

In chapter 6 we travel from the genteel courts of Europe to the harsh, sun-baked landscape of the Holy Land, which in medieval times was known as Outremer, to witness the quest of the first Crusaders and their leader, Duke Godfrey of Bouillon. This was the man whom many consider to be the archetypal Christian knight, and who waded ankle deep through the blood of thousands of slaughtered men, women, and children to become the first Latin monarch of the Holy City of Jerusalem.

It should be remembered that knights did not live and fight in isolation; there were a number of religious orders to which they belonged, and in chapter 7 we shall examine the rise and fall of the most famous of these: the Knights Templar, the Hospitalers, the Teutonic Knights, and the Knights of Calatrava. Theirs are stories of high adventure, of heroic deeds and terrible misfortune, of terror and torture, demonstrating the undeniable fact that the pursuit of wealth and worldly glory was at least as important to many as the performance of God's work.

In the final chapter and the conclusion, we will find ourselves approaching the end of the knight's story with the rise of the mercenary, the freelance fighting man who went to war not to preserve his personal liberty and possessions but rather for a steady wage. Along the way we shall meet the colorful and fascinating Englishman Sir John Hawkwood, who sold his military expertise to the highest bidder and became one of the most respected and feared generals in all of Europe. In addition to the rise of the regular army, composed mainly of infantry forces such as the formidable pikemen of Switzerland, it was the development of guns and gunpowder that sounded the death knell of the heavily armored mounted warrior, and we shall complete our portrait of the knight with a survey of the battlefield technology that ultimately made him obsolete.

This book is intended as a popular account of the history of knights and knighthood, rather than an academic study. The interested reader will find a bibliography containing the works I have found especially helpful, together with a glossary of some of the terms that were in use at the time.

1

The Mounted Warrior

The Middle Ages were characterized by wars of defense and expansion. The ninth and tenth centuries saw invasions by the Vikings and Magyars, followed later by incursions into eastern Europe by the Ottoman Turks. There were also, of course, the Norman Conquests of England and southern Italy, and the German conquests of Slav territories to the east. The period of the Crusades saw not only the Christian expeditions to the Holy Land, but also the Reconquest of Spain from the Moors. It was a time of convulsion, both politically and militarily, for the whole of Europe and the Middle East; a time of monumental power struggles between popes and emperors, between Christianity and Islam. At the center of this battle-torn landscape, drenched in the blood of millions, stood the knight. He was the paragon of virtue and the essence of war, the most powerful and deadliest element of any army.

During the medieval period, while all nobles of military age were necessarily knights, knighthood in martial terms had to be earned through some exploit involving the use of arms. Training for knighthood began at an early age. Typically the sons of nobles would be sent away at age seven to another castle to serve as a page. Pages were taught obedience and good manners, while also beginning their training in swordsmanship. At age fourteen, the youngster became a squire, whose job was to help a knight prepare for battle, maintaining both armor and weapons, and occasionally even following the knight into the battle itself.

After four years' experience of warfare, the squire could become a knight and be "dubbed." Dubbing was the ceremony in which a king or queen tapped the squire on the shoulder or neck with the flat of a sword, often following a vigil, a night of prayer and contemplation before an altar. The newly dubbed knight would fight either under his own banner (a knight banneret), or under that of another (a knight bachelor), and he would be accompanied in battle by his own pages and squires, along with other servants. In fact, the knight required the services of several attendants: one to conduct his horses; another to bear the heaviest weapons, particularly the shield or escutcheon (the origin of the French *escuyer*, esquire); one to aid him in mounting his battle horse, or to help him to his feet if dismounted; and a fourth attendant to guard prisoners, especially those of noble birth, for whom a high ransom could be expected. It is thus easy to see why the profession was a viable proposition only to those of noble birth and considerable financial resources.

At the beginning of the twelfth century, the law of primogeniture became commonly accepted by the nobility. This law entitled the eldest son of a liege lord to inherit all of his father's property. Primogeniture placed many vassals at a disadvantage in terms of land acquisition, since many of the knights whose lands were given to them by their liege lords could find themselves landless when the lord died and his son took over. This also was a tough law for the lord's other sons, who were legally entitled to little or nothing when the lord died. Since the only secure form of wealth was lordship and the possession of land and the rights of labor service from peasants, it was the dream of every lord's son to eventually own his own estate. For this reason, many younger sons set out on their own in search of wealth and glory, attending tournaments to prove their worth, and hoping that vassalage would be the first step on the road to wealth and power. They were also frequently forbidden by law to marry, since marriage might result in descendants who would dispute the landowning rights of the eldest son's descendants.

Although the word "knight" most often conjures images of the magnificent warriors and Crusaders of the medieval period, the origins of knighthood go back much farther, to ancient Rome and the *equites,* the mounted officers who held a special position in Roman society. Medieval knighthood had its roots in the Roman practice of "commendation," in which a Roman soldier would attach himself to a superior officer, pledging his military service in return for the granting of a piece of land, which was known as a *benefice.* This practice would later be taken up by great European leaders such as Charlemagne.

Each warrior who was made a lord in this manner would use the income from his land to equip himself with weapons and at least three horses: the battle horse (or *dexterarius*), which was led by hand and used only for fighting (hence the expression "to get on one's high horse" when one is ready for a confrontation); a second horse, or courser, for traveling to and from the battlefield; and finally a packhorse for his luggage.

As a landowner, the knight possessed two luxuries that ordinary peasant farmers, who had to work land that did not belong to them in order to feed their families, could only dream of: time and money. The knight's money went toward the purchase and upkeep of his battle horse and weapons; his time was spent honing the skills, in horsemanship and in fighting, that were so essential to his violent profession. Once in possession of his own area of land, a knight could do with it as he pleased, and most often he would grant pieces of it to various retainers, who would then repeat the process. The land would thus be divided over and over, until the original area was composed of small parcels, each the minimum required to support a single knight (about fifteen hundred acres).

In return for his land the knight would serve his lord with total obedience, performing a variety of duties, including fighting in the lord's army, guarding his castle, and acting as his messenger or ambassador. In fact, the knight's entire life was defined by his relationship to his lord and master, who had the final say in whom he could marry, and also in the disposition of his estate upon his death. Of course, the social hierarchy did not stop with the knight's master: the lord himself might also be a knight in the service of a higher authority, this "chain of command" only stopping at the king.

The social and economic system under which the knight operated is known as feudalism; however, this term is troublesome to say the least; there are a number of different definitions, and some historians maintain that it should be abandoned altogether. In fact, the term "feudalism" was not coined until the nineteenth century, and is analogous to the French word *féodalité*. It is commonly used to describe the features characteristic of medieval society, even if the exact nature of those features is itself a matter of considerable debate. It is quite certain, however, that the two main characteristics of society in the Middle Ages were the weakness of central government, and the performance of various services in return for fiefs (or land grants) instead of money.

Political thinking regarding these characteristics was greatly influenced by Montesquieu, who, in the eighteenth century, suggested that royal authority in France collapsed in the ninth century, and that feudalism was exported from France to England in the Norman Conquest of 1066, later spreading throughout the British Isles. However, this theory does not take account of the fact that a form of feudalism already prevailed, in which British rulers before 1066 expected political and military service from the landowning elites. Therefore, those historians who subscribe to it have had to define feudalism quite narrowly, concentrating primarily on the two social and military concepts that the Normans brought with them to England: the castle; and the feudal quota, which obliged a knight to serve his lord for forty days in every year.

During the French Revolution, the term (in its original French form) was used to describe the many abuses of the *ancien régime,* and French historians still use it in this sense. This rather loose definition is symptomatic of the many attempts that have been made to analyze and define it, attempts that are far from being closely related to one another.

Bearing these caveats in mind, let us attempt a useful definition of feudalism that will be of some help in our understanding of the society in which the knight lived and operated. The feudal society came into existence in France, Germany, the Kingdom of Burgundy-Aries, and Italy in about the tenth century. Countries that came under their influence — England, some of the Christian kingdoms of Spain, and the Latin principalities of the Near East — also possessed feudal attributes. Although there are other countries, such as Egypt and India, that displayed some analogies with feudalism in the distant past, leading some historians to label them (controversially) as feudal, the society that most closely parallels the situation in medieval Europe is Japan.

European feudalism was characterized by obligations of service (especially military service) between the vassal and his lord. In return for the vassal's service, the lord was obliged to offer protection and a livelihood to his vassal, including the land grant. In Japan the daimyos, bushi, or samurai were comparable to the vassals in Europe, and the land that was granted to them was more or less equivalent to that granted to the vassal by his lord in return for his service. In addition, an institution very close to vassalage prevailed in Russia between the thirteenth and sixteenth centuries.

In Europe the lord and the vassal were securely locked into a mutually beneficial arrangement: for the vassal there was protection and land; for the lord, there were days owed in military service, whether in battle or the garrisoning of the castle, plus counsel before embarking on an important course of action. Also among the vassal's obligations to his lord were the fee known as relief, when he received his land; the obligation to contribute to any ransom that might be demanded should his lord be captured; to contribute to his crusading expenses; and to help out when the lord's son was knighted or his daughter married. In addition, permission had to be sought if the vassal wished to marry, or to marry off his own daughter. Upon the vassal's death, his widow and children would be provided for by the lord, who would see to their education and marriage; should he die without a wife or heirs, the land would revert to the lord.

It is easy to see that feudalism was, at its center, defined by the localization of political, military, and economic power in the hands of lords and their vassals, who exercised that power from their castle headquarters, each of which held complete sway over the district in which it was situated. The resulting hierarchy resembled a pyramid, with the lowest vassals at the base and the king, of course, at the summit. This was not the case in every nation, however; in Germany, for instance, the summit of the pyramid did not reach the king, being occupied instead by the great princes.

The results of feudalism were mixed, to say the least. On the negative side, it meant that the state had a relationship with the heads of groups rather than directly with individuals farther down the social scale. Under a weak king, these men claimed sovereignty for themselves, and fought among themselves rather than allowing the state to judge their claims. This resulted in the private wars that scarred the medieval landscape. The overlords claimed numerous rights for themselves, including that of issuing private coinage, building private castles, and the power to raise taxes. Each of these manorial groups tried to be self-sufficient and to consolidate its possessions. Skirmishes and all-out wars were frequent and accounted for much of the violence, precariousness, and unpredictability of medieval life. In addition, the powers possessed by the church meant that in times of disputed succession it claimed the right not only to defend itself and maintain order, but also to nominate the ruler. This, of course, made it impossible for the church to remain impartial in matters of state, and the cause of the church frequently became identified with a particular claimant.

This must be balanced against the positive results of feudalism: for instance, the cohesion it supplied to the nations in which it operated. In the absence of any mature concept of nationality in the centuries following the fall of the Roman Empire, feudalism supplied some measure of territorial organization, linking the Germanic and Roman political systems and providing a pyramidal hierarchy that resulted in at least a nominal political and economic stability. It was also represented by the feudal bond of *legalitas,* the breaking of which was more than a felony — it was a deep dishonor. The feudal lord had conferred upon him the symbols of his high standing — his banner, lance, and shield — and these signified his protection of those who pledged their allegiance to him. For their part, his vassals swore allegiance to him on bended knee, with their hands placed between his. Neither should the protection for Europe provided by feudalism be underestimated, at a time when the Continent faced the attentions of Turks, Saracens, and Moors.

The eventual decline of feudalism occurred as a result of a number of factors, perhaps the most important of which was the impracticality of lords retaining a large number of knights who sat idle during the periods between wars. There was also the potentially serious problem of knights growing restless and bored waiting for the call to arms, which was their true vocation, and causing problems in the surrounding villages. The knights, too, found that the call to military service could come at the most inconvenient times, and for this reason the practice of commutation arose, whereby a knight would pay a sum of money (scutage) to his lord instead of going to war. Eventually money began to take the place of land as a symbol of power, and this gave rise to a new form of feudalism called bastard feudalism, a phrase coined in the late nineteenth century. Under this arrangement, lords obtained services not by granting land to tenants, but by paying annual retaining fees and daily wages. The king thus contracted with individual earls, barons, and knights to provide a fixed number of men at a fixed wage, should the need arise.

An additional blow to the pure form of feudalism came with the development of gunpowder, cannons, and firearms, which made castles and heavily armored mounted knights virtually obsolete. From the twelfth century onward, feudalism was further undermined by the rise of the centralized state, with its salaried officials and mercenary armies. Eventually the relationship between vassal and lord was replaced by that between subject and sovereign.

The Death of a Squire

Although they were literally knights in training, squires still could perform many of the feats of arms associated with their elders. On many occasions, this would result in valuable experience and honor being gained; while on others, the outcome was tragedy. The latter befell a brave and some might say foolhardy young French squire named John Boucmel in the late fourteenth century.

A company of knights from England and Navarre was making its way through France toward the town of Cherbourg, having been granted passports through the country by the constable of France, who resided at Château Josselin. Among these knights was Sir John Harlestone, governor of Cherbourg; Sir Evan Fitzwarren; Sir William Clinton; and Sir John Burley. As the evening drew in, they decided to stop for dinner at an inn close to the castle at Vannes. On hearing of the visitors' presence, the knights and squires of the castle came to visit them as brother-soldiers.

With them came John Boucmel, a squire who was renowned in the use of arms and who was in the service of John de Bourbon, count de la Marche. In the past Boucmel had often discussed the possibility of a joust with a knight who was among the visiting party, Nicholas Clifford. When he saw Clifford at the inn, Boucmel was greatly pleased, and immediately returned to the subject they had so often discussed before. "Nicholas Clifford!" he cried. "Ah! Nicholas, Nicholas, we have often wished and sought to perform a jousting match; but we never could find fit opportunity or place for it. Now, as we are here before my lord constable and these gentlemen, let us perform it; I therefore demand from you three courses with a lance."

Replied Nicholas: "John, you know that we are here but as travelers on our road, under the passport of my lord constable; what you ask of me cannot now be complied with, for I am not the principal in the passport, but under the command of these knights whom you see. If I were to stay behind, they would set out without me."

Boucmel, however, would take no refusal, crying, "Do not make such excuses as these. Let your friends be on their way, if they please, for I promise you that as soon as our tilt shall be over, I will conduct you myself within the gates of Cherbourg without loss or danger, as I can most certainly depend on my lord constable's goodwill."

Nicholas, not wishing to offend the young fellow, tried a different argument: "Now suppose it be as you say, and that I place my confidence in being safely conducted by you, yet you see we are traveling through the country without arms of any sort; therefore, even if I were willing to arm myself, I have not wherewithal to do so."

"You shall not excuse yourself that way," countered the other, "for I will tell you what I will do: I have plenty of arms at my command, and will order different sorts to be brought to the place where we shall tilt; and, when all are laid out, you shall examine them, and consider which will suit you best, for I will leave the choice to you and, when you shall have chosen, I will then arm myself."

At this point it became quite clear to Nicholas that it would not be honorable to refuse the request, so passionately was it made, and especially since the other knights had heard the entire conversation. Thus he told the squire that he would consider his request, and would give him his answer before his departure. "If it will not be possible," he added, "for me to comply with your request at this place, and if my lords, under whom I am, should be unwilling to assent to it, on my return to Cherbourg, if you will come to Valogne, and signify to me your arrival, I will immediately hasten thither, and deliver you from your engagement."

But Boucmel would not yield an inch, and replied: "Seek not for excuses: I have offered you such handsome proposals that you cannot in honor depart without running a tilt with me, according to the demand I make."

Nicholas now grew angry at the young squire's manner of speaking to him; the lad had quite clearly overstepped the mark, for although he himself had considered that it would be dishonorable to refuse the request, for the younger man himself to make such an assertion was another thing entirely. The French then returned to their castle, and were far from silent on the subject of the conversation between Nicholas Clifford and John Boucmel. When the constable himself heard of it, the French knights entreated him to allow the joust, and this he willingly promised.

When they had finished dining, the English knights and squires went to the castle to wait upon the constable, who had arranged for them an escort of seven knights who would accompany them as far as Cherbourg.

When the knights arrived at the castle to receive their escort, the constable welcomed them most warmly, and bade them stay until the following day. "Tomorrow morning, after Mass, you shall witness the combat between Nicholas Clifford and John Boucmel, and then you shall dine with me. Dinner over, you shall set out, and I will give you good guides to conduct you to Cherbourg." To this the knights agreed, and returned to their inn for the evening.

On the following morning, after Mass and confession, Clifford and Boucmel mounted their horses and rode with the English and the French to a field not far from the castle. When they had dismounted, Boucmel indicated the two suits of armor he had provided, according to his promise. When he entreated the Englishman to make his choice, the latter demurred, saying, "I will not choose; you shall have the choice." This Boucmel did, and presently both men stood armed and ready for the joust.

They mounted their horses, grasped the lances made of fine Bordeaux steel, closed the visors of their helmets, and made their way to their stations ready for the first course. Spurring their horses on, they advanced toward each other at full gallop, lowering their lances as they approached. The tip of Clifford's lance caught Boucmel high on his breastplate and was deflected off. Alas, the steel point was not deflected away harmlessly, but rather directly into the young squire's mail hood, piercing his neck clean through.

Incredibly Boucmel continued until he had reached his chair, then dismounted and sat down, as his companions rushed to his aid. Immediately the French lords took off the squire's helmet and hood, and withdrew the piece of lance from his neck. As soon as this had been done, Boucmel fell to the ground, dead.

Nicholas Clifford, on seeing what had transpired, rushed to the Frenchman in a vain attempt to offer assistance; and, when he saw that nothing more could be done, fell to the ground in inconsolable grief at the death of such a valiant young man at arms.

The constable tried to offer some comfort, saying that such things were only to be expected and, although it had turned out most unfortunately for the French squire, the Englishman could not and should not blame himself for it. Addressing the other Englishmen, the constable bade them come to dinner, and led them back to the castle in spite of their reluctance after the death of the squire. Nicholas Clifford retired to his lodgings, and refused absolutely to enter the castle, so anguished was he at the day's events. However, the constable sent for him, and thus it was impossible for him to deny this request.

When he arrived, the constable said to him: "In truth, Nicholas, I can very well believe, and I see by your looks, that you are much concerned for the death of John Boucmel; but I acquit you of it, for it was no fault of yours, and, as God is my judge, if I had been in the situation you were in, you have done nothing more than I would have done, as it is better to hurt one's enemy than to be hurt by him. Such is the fate of war."

Nicholas was hardly consoled by these well-intentioned words, but he felt able at least to remain with the company. They then dined together, and when they had finished and drunk their wine, the constable called the lord le Barrois des Barres and said to him: "Barrois, prepare yourself: I will that you conduct these Englishmen as far as Cherbourg, and that you have opened to them every town and castle, and have given to them whatever they shall be in need of."

Barrois replied that he would most willingly obey these orders.

Following this, the Englishmen returned to their quarters, where their belongings were already packed and ready. They mounted their horses and rode straight to Pontorson and Mont St. Michel, and from there to Cherbourg.

Funeral Rites

Although much missed by his comrades, the young squire John Boucmel could not have expected the funeral service of a true knight. When a man at arms died, the funeral arrangements befitted his high standing in medieval society. For an example of this, we can look to the funeral of Louis III, earl of Flanders, and his wife, the countess, in 1384. Their bodies were carried to Los, an abbey near Lille. When they were about to enter Lille, a large number of lords from France, Flanders, Hainault, and Brabant, who had arrived on the eve of the funeral, went to meet the bodies at the Gate of the Invalids, and carry them through the town to the Church of St. Peter.

All of the knights and their squires were armed as for war, and were followed by their banners and the barons who assisted in carrying the earl's body through the town. The barons were Sir John de Vienne, admiral of France, on the right, and the lord de Guistelles on the left; then Sir Valeran de Ravenal on the right, the castellan of Disquenieu on the left; and finally the lord d'Estournay on the right, and Sir Ansel de Salins on the left.

Those barons who carried the body of the countess were the lord de Sully on the right, and the lord de Châtillon on the left; Sir Guy de Pontalliers, marshal of Burgundy, on the right and Sir Guy de Guistelles on the left; then Sir Henry du Coing on the right, and the castellan of Furnes on the left.

Once within the walls of the Church of St. Peter, the obsequies were performed by other nobles; the earl's shields that accompanied them were supported by their squires during the Mass. In book II, chapter 147 of his *Chronicles,* Froissart (who was on friendly terms with many of the great and good of Europe and who might be described as the Continent's first celebrity interviewer) describes the convoy thus:

First, the duke of Burgundy by himself, and the first shield was borne before him, which shield was supported by the lord de Ravenal, by the lord de la Gouneuse, by Labequin de la Coutre, and by John de Pontalliers, brother to the marshal of Burgundy. The second shield was borne before my lord John of Artois, Count d'Eu, and the lord Philip de Bar, by Valeran de la

Sale and Lesclaus d'Annequin. Next followed the count de la Marche and the lord d'Artois; the shield was borne by Gillon de Labert and Robin de Florigny. Then came Sir Robert de Namur, and with him his nephew Sir William de Namur; the shield was borne by Chaux Bernard and Girard de Sternaille. . . .

Then came those who were to make offerings of the warhorses of the earl: first my lord de Châtillon and Sir Simon de Lalain, bailiff of Hainault. These lords were on foot, and the horse was armed and caparisoned; with the second horse were Sir Valeran de Ravenal and the castellan de Dixmude; with the third, Sir Hugh de Melun and the lord d'Aucy; the lord de Burnel and the lord de Brumeu were with the fourth horse. Then came those who were to offer the steeds of the convoy: first, Sir Henry d'Ancoing and Sir Gerard de Guistelles; with the second, the lord de Montigny and the lord de Rasenghien; the lord de la Haurade and the castellan de Furnes were with the third; and the fourth had the lord de Saugmelles and Sir Rowland de la Clicque.

Following the procession of the earl's horses, other nobles carried his swords of war, his battle helmets, and finally his banners. When the obsequies were ended, the earl was laid in the ground by Sir John de Vienne, admiral of France; Lord de Guistelle, Sir Valeran de Ravenal, the castellan de Dixmude, the lord de Ray, and Sir Ansel de Salins. The body of the countess was interred by Sir Guy de la Trimouille, the lord de Châtillon, the lord Gerard de Guistelles, Sir Henry d'Antoing, and the castellan of Furnes.

Froissart states:

It should be observed that all who officially entered the Church of St. Peter at Lille, with the corpse in the evening, remained there until the Mass of the morrow, as well as those knights who were armed, as those who bore the banners and the squires who led the horses. There were about four hundred men, clothed in black, appointed to carry the body of the earl and countess of Flanders, through Lille, to the Church of St. Peter, and each of them bore a torch in his hand. These four hundred men held their torches on the morrow in the church during Mass, and they were all of them officers in the principal towns or of the earl's household.

The Mass was celebrated by the archbishop of Rheims, assisted by the bishops of Paris, Tournay, Cambray, and Arras, and by five abbots. During the obsequies, seven hundred candles burned around the earl's body, casting their flickering light on the five banners that covered the catafalque. In the center was the banner of Flanders; on the right, that of Artois; on the left, that of Boulogne. The fourth was of Nevers, and the fifth of Rethel.

A magnificent dinner was then provided for the mourners, all of whom were given the black clothes they had worn. When the ceremony was finally at an end, they all returned to their homes.

2

From Blood to Laughter

One of the most potent and romantic images of knighthood is that of bold, armor-clad warriors competing at lavish tournaments, cheered on by elegant and beautifully attired ladies. While this image is certainly accurate, it is not always appreciated that the origin of these genteel affairs lay in violent and bloody practice battles in which it was not uncommon for knights to be killed. The reason for this is quite simple: the knights were essentially a mounted combat force whose success depended on their fighting skills as well as their ability to work together. Naturally this took a good deal of practice, and the early tournaments were means by which the knights' skills and battle tactics could be honed to perfection. They were also proving grounds for knights offering their services.

These practice battles were waged over miles of open countryside between two groups of fighters, and were not regulated or mediated by any official. Other than an area called a recess, where knights could take temporary refuge, there were no safeguards. Unlike the gladiators of ancient Rome, who practiced against each other with relatively harmless wooden swords, the medieval knights used the armor and weapons they would employ in a real battle against an enemy force.

A knight could make or lose a fortune at one of these tournaments. If he lost, he would have to pay the victor a large ransom, which usually included his armor, weapons, and horse — in short, his most valuable and essential possessions. The tournaments were also hugely important in terms of a knight's career: if he fought with skill and courage, he might be spotted by a lord on the lookout for good soldiers. Of course, the opposite also was true: a knight was only as good as his last battle, and if he performed poorly, his position in his lord's army might well be seriously diminished — assuming he survived.

The early tournaments were not mock battles; the fighting was for real, and the stakes were high. Chivalry did not apply, and no one even attempted to avoid killing an opponent. Indeed, some knights practiced the very sly "count of Flanders" technique, whereby they would wait until late in the day when most knights were fatigued from combat, and then attack them, scoring easy victories over their worn-out fellows and claiming their possessions.

Such was the rate of injury and death during these tournaments that the church tried to ban them, threatening to deny Christian burial to any knight killed during one. However, this proved no deterrent to knights who were looking for work, or who were simply addicted to the bloody excitement of battle. Many English knights traveled to France in search of tournaments in which to fight. The church was not alone in its dislike of tournaments. Princes and kings also were concerned at the high financial cost in terms of injury and death, both of men and horses. Not only did they need skilled and healthy men to fight for them in important battles and sieges, but also many leaders suspected that the tournaments might be fertile grounds for insurrection and treachery.

And so, in the last decade of the twelfth century, King

Richard I attempted to control and regulate the tournaments by devising a licensing system. In 1194 licenses were issued for five locations in England. Knights who wanted to participate in a tournament had to pay a fee, and foreign knights were banned from attending. In this way Richard was able to observe any political scheming and also to raise money for his military campaigns.

Gradually the tournaments became safer: the violent and chaotic melee was replaced by one-to-one battles, which better demonstrated the knights' horsemanship. Eventually these single combats evolved into the joust. What had begun in the gore and death of the battlefield was ultimately transformed into an elegant, charming, and splendid entertainment watched by noble ladies and children, at which minstrels played and danced and sumptuous banquets were given.

When jousting knights used the lance, a weapon specifically designed for mounted combat; although, in keeping with the greater emphasis on safety in the sport, the lance would sometimes be fitted with a three-pronged tip called a coronal, which dispersed the energy of the impact, preventing the weapon from piercing an opponent's armor and causing serious injury or death.

Different types of armor also were developed for jousting: some had heavier protection on the side facing the opponent, while other suits were equipped with a built-in shield at one side of the waist, at the point where the lance was supposed to strike. Yet another type of armor was designed to break apart on impact, leaving the rider safe in the saddle.

In the early jousts knights would simply ride their horses at full gallop toward one another and attempt to knock each other to the ground. In the mid-fifteenth century, however, another safety innovation was introduced. The tilt barrier began simply as a rope hung with fabric, which was stretched along the jousting ground. Each rider was supposed to keep to his side of this four-foot-high barrier. However, something a little stronger and more resilient was needed, so the rope was eventually replaced with a wooden barrier up to six feet high. The purpose of the tilt barrier was to force the jousters to point their lances at an angle as they approached each other, thus making the weapons more likely to break on impact and less likely to cause serious injury to an opponent.

During tournaments the spectators could watch a variety of other displays of the knights' skill, including the ring, in which a knight would ride toward a dangling hoop a few inches in diameter and attempt to catch it upon his lance. In another game, the quintain, the knight would ride at a dummy that held a target in one hand and a counterweight in the other. This game tested speed as well as accuracy, for as soon as the target was hit, the dummy would spin around and the counterweight would strike a slow rider on the head, causing much hilarity among the crowd.

The origin of the expression "to wear your heart on your sleeve" can be found in the joust, and the custom wherein a lady would bestow a favor (usually a scarf or a ribbon) upon the knight representing her in a tournament. The knight would attach the favor to his left arm, so that all might see the object of his devotion.

Jean Froissart, one of the greatest chroniclers of medieval times, had much to say on the subject of tournaments. He was born at Valenciennes, France, in 1337, and his family were members of the bourgeoisie, but his passion for the arts propelled him into far loftier social circles. The *Chronicles*, for which he is remembered, were begun when he was only twenty years old, and he continued to expand and revise them throughout his life. In 1361 he traveled to England, entered the church, and secured an introduction to Queen Philippa of Hainault, wife of Edward III, who made him her secretary and clerk of her chapel.

Most of his life was spent traveling throughout Europe, his many and varied experiences faithfully recorded in his *Chronicles*, and based either on what he had seen with his own eyes, or on the firsthand testimonies he received from the knights and mercenaries he befriended and who were his patrons. His great love was the colorful pageantry of medieval life, particularly the excitement and chivalry of the tournament. Although there are many occasions when Froissart is less than accurate (he was unswervingly sympathetic to his lordly patrons, for instance, even when they committed horrible atrocities during sieges), he nevertheless offers a dramatic and vivid picture of life in his period. For this reason I believe we can safely turn to Thomas Johnes's 1805 translation of Froissart's exciting account of a tournament held in France over a period of four days in May 1390, for a taste of the pomp and splendor of these events.

The Tournament at St. Inglevert

The three knights who held the tournament at St. Inglevert, near Calais, were Sir Boucicaut the Younger, Sir Reginald de Roye, and Lord de Saimpi. They had let it be known that they would remain there for thirty days to test the resolve of all comers. Word of the tournament had spread throughout Europe, and especially in England, where a number of knights and squires decided it would be sorely remiss of them to pass up such an exciting and worthy challenge. Chief among these were Sir John Holland, earl of Huntingdon; Sir Peter Courtenay; Sir John Traicton; Sir John Goulouffre; Sir John Rousseau; Sir Thomas Scorabonne; Sir William Cliseton; Sir William Clinton; Sir William Taillebourg; Sir Godfrey de Seton; Sir William de Haquenay; Sir John Bolton; Sir John Arundel; Sir John d'Ambreticourt; and Sir Henry Beaumont. In all, more than one hundred knights and squires journeyed across the English Channel to meet the challenge, saying, "Let us prepare ourselves to attend this tournament near Calais; for these French knights only hold it that they may have our company: it is well done, and shows they do not want courage; let us not disappoint them!"

Plans for the tournament were so widely known that many people who had no intention of actually participating nevertheless crossed the Channel to view the proceedings, while the knights and squires themselves sent ahead their weapons and other equipment to Calais in preparation. The three French knights made their way first to Boulogne, and from there to the monastery of St. Inglevert, where they received the pleasing news that their challenge had been taken up most handsomely by a large number of English knights, who were even then on their way to Calais.

In response, the French knights gave orders for three vermillion-colored pavilions to be pitched at the site of the tournament. Before each pavilion one of the knights had his coat of arms placed, so whoever might wish to engage him in combat need only touch it (or have his squire do so).

Monday

On May 21, 1390, the English knights set out from Calais to St. Inglevert. On their arrival, they found all the preparations in order, and gazed with satisfaction upon the lush green of the field on which the tournament was to be conducted. The proceedings were opened by Sir John Holland, who sent his squire to touch the war target of Sir Boucicaut. The French knight immediately emerged from his pavilion, ready for battle. Both mounted their warhorses, took their lances in a resolute grip, and faced each other in silence for several seconds before spurring their mounts on at full gallop toward one another. Such was the force with which they met that Boucicaut's lance penetrated Holland's shield and thrust along the English knight's arm. His armor saved him, however, and he was uninjured. This was a splendid opening to the proceedings, and the spectators applauded enthusiastically. At the second course, however, they passed each other with only slight contact; and their horses refused to complete the third. Although Sir John Holland was anxious to meet his adversary again, Sir Boucicaut let it be known that he had no intention of tilting again with the Englishman that day.

Holland accepted this with good grace, and sent his squire to touch the target of Lord de Saimpi, who emerged from his pavilion and took his lance and shield. Spurring their horses violently toward each other, they met in the middle of the course, de Saimpi's lance striking Holland's helmet and knocking it clean off. Holland returned to his countrymen, who rehelmed him, and both knights took up their lances once again. They met at full gallop, this time the lance of each knight striking his opponent's shield with such force that each would surely have been thrown from his horse had not the intense pressure of their legs against their mounts' sides kept them securely in their saddles. Nevertheless, the shock of the powerful contact was so great that each knight took a few moments to refresh himself and to get his breath.

In spite of their fatigue the two knights were anxious to have at each other once again, and, their refreshment taken, they spurred their horses on toward each other. This time the tip of each lance found the opponent's helmet, the contact causing fiery sparks to fly from the tempered steel. And this time Lord de Saimpi was unhelmed. The spectators were more than satisfied with this tilt, and commented most favorably on the skill and bravery of the three knights who had opened the tournament. Sir John Holland let it be known that he wished to joust yet again in honor of his lady; however, he had already completed the six allotted courses, and so with good grace he quit to make room for others who had yet to prove themselves that day.

It was now the turn of the valiant Nicholas Clifford, now a lord, who sent his squire to place his rod against the war shield of Sir Boucicaut. Immediately, Boucicaut appeared from his pavilion and mounted the horse that had been made ready for him. They met each other at full gallop, and once again the fire flew from their helmets into the clear May air. This was a perfect course: neither lance was broken; neither knight lost his stirrups or his helmet, and both returned to their places to make ready for the second course.

This time Sir Boucicaut came off worse, breaking his lance and losing his helmet. Although Clifford was ready for another tilt, the French knight did not replace his helmet; and so, anxious to continue, Clifford sent to touch the shield of Lord de Saimpi. This knight was ready for his opponent and spurred his horse full at the Englishman, who broke his lance in three places upon de Saimpi's shield, losing his own helmet in the exchange. The spectators showed their approval of Lord Clifford's performance, maintaining that he had most bravely and honorably comported himself, and so he tilted no more that day.

Now Sir Henry Beaumont came forward, sending his squire to touch the shield of Sir Boucicaut. The French knight had not yet dismounted following his encounter with Lord Clifford and so was quite ready for the challenge. At their first course, however, Beaumont's aim was not particularly good, and for this he paid a price. While the tip of his lance merely grazed Boucicaut's side, the French knight's lance struck him full in the center of his shield, knocking him brutally from his saddle to the ground. Beaumont's attendants instantly rushed to his aid, raising him and helping him to remount. The following two courses were conducted with great skill and without injury to either knight.

At this point there came a great surprise to everyone. Sir Peter Courtenay, in a display of considerable enthusiasm, sent a squire to touch the war shields of all three of the French knights. He was immediately asked his intentions, and he replied that he wished to tilt twice with each knight. Somewhat bemused, the Frenchmen nevertheless acceded to his request, Sir Reginald de Roye offering himself first. They charged at each other, aiming their lances with the utmost care and precision; unfortunately, on this occasion their mounts did not share their enthusiasm, and due to their restiveness, the knights missed each other completely. On the second course, Sir Reginald managed to strike off his opponent's helmet and thus retreated to his pavilion, his obligation now met.

Taking his place, Lord de Saimpi issued forth to face the valiant Englishman, and on their first course each lance was shattered. Barely pausing to receive new lances, they launched themselves at each other again. This time Courtenay's horse swerved a little at the last moment, giving his opponent the opportunity to strike — but it was Courtenay's lance that found its target, striking the Frenchman's helmet from his head.

Finally it was Sir Boucicaut's turn, and on their first course they struck each other on the shield with such force that their horses were stopped in their tracks, coming to a shuddering, snorting halt. On the second course they managed to unhelmet each other. With the six courses now complete, Courtenay requested the favor of being allowed to run one more course with any of the French knights who pleased. However, he was politely told that he had done enough that day, and so withdrew.

Next came Sir John Goulouffre, who sent his squire to touch the shield of Sir Reginald de Roye. Their meeting, however, passed without remarkable event: on the first course, they hit each other's helmets; their horses refused to run the second; at the third tilt they broke each other's lance; on the fourth they passed without landing a blow; and on the fifth both were unhelmeted, and each retired to his party.

Sir John Rousseau, famous in many countries for his expertise and bravery, chose Lord de Saimpi. On the first course they met each other with such force that they were compelled to stop, and so they returned to their posts in preparation for the second. This time their horses swerved at the last moment and they missed each other altogether, which caused both a good deal of annoyance. The third course yielded far better results, for the lance point of each man found his opponent's helmet, and struck with such power that the visor of each flew away in a shower of sparks.

Sir Peter Shirbourne, a young and relatively inexperienced knight — but one not lacking in courage — chose to face Sir Boucicaut. As had happened before in this tournament, the swerving of the horses meant that the first course passed entirely without incident. This was not to last, however, for, each being determined to make a better show at the second tilt, they spurred their horses furiously at one another, each receiving a powerful blow upon the visor. Sir Boucicaut broke his lance, but not so the young Englishman, and Boucicaut's helmet flew from his head amid a livid spray of crimson blood that issued from his nose.

It was now nearly vespers, the sixth canonical hour, but Sir Peter Shirbourne would not be satisfied until he had completed his number of courses, and sent his squire to touch the shield of Lord de Saimpi. They rode at each other with tremendous force, their lance points glancing off the top of each other's helmet. It was generally agreed among the spectators that this had been a fortunate thing, for such had been their speed that, had their lances been pointed lower and found their shields, the force would surely have caused them serious injury. On the next course they broke their lances into three parts on each other's shields, the English knight losing his saddle and plummeting to the ground. Although unhurt, Shirbourne returned with his attendants to the other Englishmen, and it was decided that the day's jousts were at an end.

The English knights rode back to Calais and their inns, where, together with the people who had accompanied them to France, they passed the rest of the evening in animated discussion of the day's events. Their French opponents returned to St. Inglevert with their own supporters to hold forth with each other on similar topics.

Tuesday

The morning was bright and warm, perfect weather for the noble sport that was to continue that day. After Mass, the

English set out once again from Calais, and arrived at St. Inglevert to find the French ready and waiting for them. The first few meetings passed much as they had done the previous day, with the knights from each country acquitting themselves with skill and valor.

About midway through the morning, Sir Godfrey de Seton presented himself, and sent his squire to touch the shield of Sir Reginald de Roye. The French knight was already mounted, and so came forward immediately. The first course saw their lances find each other's shield, striking with such force that their powerful horses were halted. The knights did not drop their lances, but bore them proudly back to their posts to make ready for the second course. This time their horses swerved, causing them to miss their targets and drop their lances, which were immediately returned to them by their attendants. Many among the spectators commented that the knights seemed extraordinarily heated.

On the third course Sir Godfrey dealt Sir Reginald a severe blow, which landed on the top of the French knight's helmet, and thus did him no harm. But Sir Reginald, who was considered to be among the most powerful and skillful knights in France, and who also was driven by the love of a certain young lady whom he prized above all other things, struck at his opponent's shield with such force and accuracy that his lance pierced it, breaking in two on contact. As the butt fell to the ground, the lance tip lay embedded in the shield, and the metal of the shield flowered inward and entered the English knight's left arm.

In spite of his agonizing wound Sir Godfrey did not fail to finish his course. His friends came to his aid immediately, helping him from his horse, pulling the lance tip from his ruined shield and the pieces of shield from his arm. The flow of blood that splashed upon the knight's armor was stopped, and the arm was well bandaged. Both the French and the English praised Sir Reginald for his skill, no one even thinking to criticize him for wounding his opponent. This, after all, was the nature of their calling; and even in a friendly encounter such as this, injuries were only to be expected.

Later in the day a young and richly armed English knight named Thomelin Messidon, anxious to gain honor for himself, sent his squire to touch the shield of Sir Boucicaut, who came forward immediately. After an indifferent first tilt, they spurred at each other again, and this time Thomelin Messidon shivered his lance into fragments, while his opponent's found its target squarely and with such force that it lifted the young Englishman clean over the crupper of his horse to the ground. Messidon's assistants instantly ran to him and, finding that he was in no fit state to stand up, let alone continue jousting that day, carried him off.

Vowing revenge for his comrade, another English squire, named Navarton, immediately came forward and touched Boucicaut's shield. The French knight was ready for the challenge, and the two charged at each other, striking each other on the visors of their helmets but doing no other damage. After having their helmets readjusted by their attendants, they rode at each other again, this time their lances finding their targets and halting their horses in their tracks. On the third course Navarton hit Boucicaut hard upon his shield, but in return received a blow that unhelmeted him. This done, Boucicaut withdrew to his friends, it being decided that he had done sufficient for that day.

The final tilt of the day was performed by another English squire, named Sequaqueton, who sent to touch the shield of Sir Reginald de Roye. On the first course the Englishman received a blow that threw him quite violently backward upon the crupper of his horse, and the spectators were most impressed when he managed to stay mounted and finish the course. On the second course their lances found each other's helmet, and again the sparks flew into the warm air. The third tilt saw Sequaqueton badly unhelmeted, with such force that even his horse staggered and almost fell to the ground. Nevertheless the young Englishman conducted himself extremely well, and, as it was now late, it was decided that the day's proceedings should end.

Wednesday

The weather was kind to them again the following day, and in the warm sunshine the jousting began with a young English squire named John Savage, squire of honor to the earl of Huntingdon, who sent to touch the shield of Sir Reginald de Roye. The knights rode at each other with such great speed, and found each other's shields with such accuracy that, had their lances not shattered on impact, they both would surely have been thrown violently to the ground. Indeed, such was the force of the impact that each knight bore in his shield his opponent's lance tip, and for some moments the spectators thought they must be witnessing a repeat of the unfortunate events that befell Sir Godfrey de Seton the previous day. However, when examined by his friends, each knight was found to be unhurt, which caused much joy on both sides.

Although they were told that they had done enough that day, and would not be required to joust again, John Savage let it be known that he was far from satisfied, saying he had not crossed the sea to France for a single joust. When Sir Reginald heard this, he was impressed, and replied that Savage was right, that he should be gratified either by Sir Reginald or one of his companions. After a short rest, the two knights charged at each other twice more, first missing each other due to the swerving of their mounts, and then managing to unhelmet each other, much to the appreciation of the spectators. Savage was assured that he had performed most honorably, but now it was time to make way for others. To this he agreed, and joined the spectators.

Later that day a knight from Ostrevant in Hainault, who had been educated in England, came forward. His name was Sir John d'Ambreticourt, brother to the famous Sir Eustace d'Ambreticourt. He sent his squire to touch the war shield of Sir Reginald de Roye. Having taken their stations, the two knights charged at one another, their lances causing fiery sparks to fly from their shields. Their second course was yet more powerful and skillful; indeed, such was the force with which lance met shield that their horses were compelled to rear up on their haunches, and for a moment the spectators thought that they must surely be unhorsed. Their only loss, however, was their lances, which they were both forced to drop. Their third course saw the first serious incident of the tournament, as Sir Reginald was violently unhelmeted and badly injured about the head — so badly, in fact, that he was unable to tilt again that day.

As the unfortunate Sir Reginald was carried away by his friends, Sir John, anxious for another tilt, touched the shield of Sir Boucicaut, who advanced immediately. Sparks again flew from shields as they met on the first course. The second course saw their lances glance threateningly off their helmets, but no harm was done. On what was to be their final course that day, both were quite violently unhelmeted, although not as violently as had been poor Sir Reginald; and following this, it was decided that the day's proceedings should end.

Thursday

The English rode out once again from Calais, looking forward to another fine day of skillful and valorous tilting. It was not to be, however, due to the ignoble behavior of one knight, a Bohemian named Sir Herchauce, of the household of the queen of England. When asked with whom he wished to tilt, Herchauce replied that he chose Sir Boucicaut.

The trouble arose on their very first course, which gave every indication of demonstrating a fine and skillful tilt. However, Sir Herchauce waited until the two knights had moved out of the line of tilting before landing his opponent a stout blow on the helmet. This was a disgraceful display and, should the Frenchman have chosen to do so, he would have been completely within his rights to demand as forfeit the Bohemian's arms and horse.

The proceedings were halted while a lengthy discussion ensued between the English and the French. In truth, the English knew full well that their comrade had acted without honor, and it was only due to the French knights' pardoning of the act that Herchauce avoided walking home. Herchauce knew himself that he had performed very badly, and begged as a favor to be allowed to run one more course. When asked with whom he wished to tilt, he sent his squire to touch the shield of Sir Reginald de Roye, who had received such a violent blow the previous day but who was now sufficiently recovered to ride again.

Sir Reginald agreed to the challenge, mounted his horse, and moved to his station facing the Bohemian. Both knights spurred their horses simultaneously, their lances striking each other's shield squarely. Sir Reginald, however, was by far the better tilter, and the force of his lance's impact thrust Herchauce clean out of his saddle, to land ignominiously on the ground. His attendants raised him and helped him back to the English, who were well pleased with what had happened to him, considering it just recompense for his earlier uncourteous behavior.

More palatable matters now ensued with the arrival of a squire named John Merlan, who sent to touch the war target of Sir Reginald de Roye. Answering that he was at the young man's service, Sir Reginald took his station, and the two flew at each other, their lances giving violent blows to their helmets. Without injury they commenced the second course, this time the force of lances upon shields halting their steeds in their tracks. Sir Reginald prevailed at the third course, forcing the young squire from his saddle and to the ground, where his fellows came to his aid.

There followed another squire, named John Mouton, who

chose Sir Boucicaut as adversary. The older knight's experience and skill won out in the end, however, for after two relatively uneventful courses, Boucicaut unhelmeted the young Englishman, who retired to his fellows.

The spectators then murmured their appreciation as a very handsome young Englishman named Jaquemin Strop appeared. Sitting most nobly upon his horse, he sent for the target of Lord de Saimpi to be indicated. On their first course their horses veered away from the tilt line and the knights missed each other, which caused them both some annoyance. The second course saw fire issue from their helmets as each man's lance found its target, although neither helmet was lost. Lord de Saimpi prevailed at the third course, for his opponent's lance shattered on contact with his shield, and he was able to unhorse the young Englishman.

Later in the day a very elegant young squire named Nicholas Lamb, anxious to prove his skill in arms, also indicated that he would like to tilt against Lord de Saimpi, who was already mounted and who readily agreed to the challenge. His alacrity, indeed, was quite in evidence as he grasped his lance from his attendant and fairly flew to his station to prepare for the first tilt. The two knights met with such speed and ferocity that their lances shivered into fragments, although both were unhurt and remained in their saddles. On the second course the fire flew from their helmets but they remained intact, and the spectators roared their appreciation of this fine display.

The knights then rested a few moments, and while they did so eyed each other intently, to ascertain where they could best place their lances at the moment of contact. The result was a perfect display of tilting, for as they spurred their horses toward each other they aimed with the greatest finesse, each knight hitting the upper part of his opponent's helmet at the same instant. The contact was so neat and so well timed that the lacings burst and the helmets flew gracefully over the cruppers of the horses and onto the field.

As it turned out, no more knights appeared on the English side, and so the tournament was judged to have come to a perfect end. The earl of Huntingdon, Lord Clifford, Lord Beaumont, Sir John Clifton, Sir John d'Ambreticourt, and all the other knights who had attended, waited together on the French knights and thanked them most warmly for receiving them over the past days.

Said the English knights: "All the knights who have accompanied us have now tilted, we take our leave of you, and return to Calais on our way to England. We know well that whoever may wish to try their skill in arms will find you here for thirty days according to your proclamation. On our return to England, we shall loudly speak of your gallantry, and tell all those who may inquire of these deeds of arms to come and witness them in person."

Their French hosts replied: "Many thanks, they shall be made welcome, and delivered by deeds of arms as you have been; and we desire you will accept our best acknowledgments for the courtesy you have shown us."

Thus in a most friendly and courteous manner did the English and French knights take leave of each other, the former stopping briefly at Calais before taking passage boats to Dover, landing there at about midday on Saturday. They stayed there until after Mass on Sunday and then made their way to Rochester, where they stayed the night. They reached London together and then separated, each continuing the journey to his own home.

From the time the English left for Calais, Froissart claims never to have heard of any other knight arriving to challenge the three valiant Frenchmen, who remained at St. Inglevert for the remainder of the thirty days, and then made their leisurely way home.

3

The Knight's Equipment

ife in medieval Europe was characterized to a large
extent by extreme violence and the need to protect
oneself, one's family, and one's land from the attentions of aggressors. It need hardly be mentioned that the
weaponry created and used by any culture is totally dependent on the level of technology and materials to which it has
access; and the Middle Ages saw considerable advances in
weapons design and construction, in addition to the tactics
with which they were deployed. As we shall see in this chapter, the weaponry available to the medieval knight was both
varied and terrifyingly effective.

Swords

Although there have obviously been many different types of
swords used throughout history, the sword that is most
closely identified with the medieval knight is the longsword,
also known as the warsword. This fearsome weapon was long-
bladed, double-edged, and straight-hilted, and was used
throughout Europe in the Middle Ages. Especially favored
by knights fighting in the Crusades, it took considerable

strength by the wielder to use it effectively; but effective and versatile it most certainly was, being used to both thrust and slash. It was so heavy that it could even be used to split armor, leaving an enemy stunned and almost defenseless. In addition, the pommel of the sword (the rounded projection at the end of the grip) could be used to attack an opponent in close quarters fighting, and this is the origin of the phrase "to pummel someone."

A type of sword commonly used in Europe in the fourteenth and fifteenth centuries was the bastard, or hand and a half sword. Long and straight-bladed, the bastard sword could be used to either thrust or slash. It featured a long grip, which allowed the weapon to be used with either one or two hands. Both of its names derive from the fact that the grip was not quite long enough to accommodate two hands comfortably: there was really only room for one and a half hands. Thus it was somewhere between a one- and two-handed weapon; in other words, a "bastard."

Perhaps because of its name, most people tend to associate the broadsword with the great Crusading period of the eleventh and twelfth centuries. As we have just noted, however, the weapon of choice at that time was the longsword. The broadsword was actually not in extensive use until the seventeenth century, and its name is somewhat misleading, for the blade was rarely wider than two inches. However, the name does not describe it with reference to swords in general, but to the very thin-bladed rapier that had been fashionable in the previous century. The broadsword had a straight, single-edged blade, and a basket hilt, rather than the cross hilt favored in earlier times. The narrowness of its blade (and that of the rapier) was a result of the increased use of firearms and artillery on the battlefield, making the brute power of the longsword obsolete.

The greatsword could be described as the king of swords, a truly impressive and frightening weapon weighing up to twenty pounds and capable of crushing heavy armor with ease. In Germany it was called the *zweihander*, meaning "two-handed," and it required both hands and considerable upper-body strength to wield properly. The greatsword was not a thrusting weapon; its long, straight blade was designed for swinging, and with its weight it could quite easily sever arms, legs, and heads. Like the longsword, however, the greatsword was rendered obsolete by the development of firearms and the resulting disappearance of heavy armor in the late sixteenth century.

Finally there was the shortsword, the descendant of the Greek *kopis* and Roman *gladius*. Shortswords were longer than daggers but shorter than longswords, and were much favored in the Middle Ages as both primary and backup weapons. Apart from their usefulness to warriors of lesser strength, they were also used by knights wielding longswords in close quarters battle: the shortsword could be used to strike at the torso of an enemy who had his arms upraised to block the blow from a longsword. Shortswords were also carried as backup weapons by spearmen and archers.

The Bow

One of the oldest weapons in the arsenal of humanity, the use of the bow and arrow for hunting and war dates back to the Paleolithic period, when it appeared in Africa, Asia, and Europe. Arrowheads were originally of wood, then of stone, bone, or metal; the bow itself was composed of various woods and bone, while the bowstring was usually made of flax, hemp, silk, cotton, or sinew. Tension energy was created by bending the bow and attaching the string to each end; the energy was increased by pulling the string back, and released by releasing the string, thus propelling the arrow with much greater speed and accuracy than could be achieved merely by throwing it. At this stage in its development, the bow was an extremely useful but not particularly powerful weapon. This changed with the invention of the composite bow on the steppes of Central Asia in about 1500 B.C.

The composite bow was made of various materials, among them wood, bone, horn, and sinew, glued together in three layers. These materials would be added to a three-piece wood core, each layer increasing the strength and elasticity of the weapon. Strips of horn would be attached to the belly (the side facing the archer), and a length of sinew would be glued to the back. The elasticity thus achieved greatly increased the range of the bow, which could be up to four hundred yards.

The longbow was used in Wales in the twelfth century, and became widely used in the Welsh wars of Edward I in the late thirteenth century. These weapons required great strength and skill to master; the bow was the height of the archer, and the arrows about half that. The string required at least a hundred foot-pounds of pressure just to draw it, let alone aim it accurately. As might be expected, the greater length of the bow and bowstring meant that this weapon had a much greater range and power than its smaller cousin. Made of a single piece of wood (yew was most favored), the longbow proved itself most effective in its deployment at the Battles of Crécy, Poitiers, and Agincourt, in which English longbowmen caused a huge number of casualties among their French opponents from several hundred yards away.

In response to the weapon's success, particularly at the Battle of Agincourt, the French would cut off the index and middle fingers of any English longbowmen they captured, thus making it impossible for them ever to use the weapon again. Naturally appalled by this behavior, the English bowmen from then on would display their index and middle fingers across the battlefield at their French enemies. This is the origin of the British insult of putting two fingers up at someone, a gesture more or less equivalent to the American middle-finger gesture.

The composite bow and the longbow were fantastically successful weapons. They were relatively easy to produce, and with their rapid rate of fire were used long after the introduction of guns, which were difficult to manufacture, took a good deal of time to load, and often failed altogether.

The Crossbow

Although used in Roman times, the crossbow (or arbalest) was not widely used in Europe until well into the medieval period. Like the simple bow before it, the crossbow was originally constructed of wood (mainly yew), but later incorporated sinew in the frame to increase strength and elasticity. At first, crossbows were not particularly effective weapons, being slow to load and prone to misfiring. As their design and construction improved, however, so did their popularity. And that popularity is entirely understandable: the tension energy in the bowstring was not held by the firer's arm, but by a metal nut that was released by pressing the long, curved trigger. This allowed the weapon to be aimed at one's leisure, although its considerable weight was a drawback.

An arbalester (crossbowman) was able to fire, on average, only one bolt per six fired by an archer. In addition, the range of crossbows was not particularly impressive, and in wet conditions their sinew bowstrings were useless. Reloading was a fairly elaborate affair. Early crossbows had a stirrup on the front of the stock; to reload, the arbalester placed the weapon vertically on the ground and his foot through the stirrup, pulling the bowstring back until it was caught in a notch in the nut. Later, aids to reloading were developed, leading to the ratchet and rolling purchase crossbows, which used elaborate levers, gears, and pulleys to draw back the string. These crossbows could be used by sick or injured men, or even by children.

Interestingly the crossbow was banned by the church at the Lateran Council of 1139, which considered it too inhumane to be used by Christians against Christians. The military historian Philip Warner makes a wry comment on this subject in his book *The Medieval Castle:* "In the eleventh century it was fair to chop a man to pieces with an axe but not fair to shoot him from a distance. In the twentieth century it is unfair to poison his drinking water but quite legitimate to blow him to pieces."

Although the crossbow was more powerful than bows and longbows, the time it took to reload, its weight, and its susceptibility to wet weather conditions made it a less than ideal weapon, especially compared to the longbow, as the Genoese arbalesters discovered to their considerable cost when engaging English longbowmen at the Battle of Crécy in 1346.

The Ax

Axes, like bows and arrows, are among the most ancient of human weapons, dating to the flint hand axes of the Neolithic period. Early axes were constructed with a wooden haft and a stone or bone head. While cavalry soldiers used long-handled axes in the Middle Ages, their most popular form was the pole ax, or halberd, essentially an ax head mounted on the end of a long pole.

One-handed axes were most commonly used in combat situations, and were favored for the ease with which they could be used to hack and slice through one's opponents, splitting armor and cleaving flesh and bone. Battle-axes were simply larger, double-headed versions that could be wielded with two hands and that required an enormous amount of strength and stamina. Consequently these weapons were not used nearly as frequently as their smaller, lighter cousins. In Europe battle-axes tended to have socketed heads into which the haft fit, as opposed to the two components simply being lashed together, their handles reinforced against the shocks of battle.

Hammers, Mauls, and Mattocks

The medieval war hammer was another terrifyingly efficient and versatile weapon, which included a sharp projection that could puncture and rip open plate armor, and a heavy, blunt component that could deliver deadly blows. Such was the weight of the hammer head that when the blade was brought down upon a foe, even the extremely tough and resilient chain mail was often no match (see chapter 5). Some versions of this fearsome weapon even had a spear tip attached to the end of the wooden haft, so that it could also be used for thrusting and stabbing. The hafts were reinforced with metal bars running their length.

A less sophisticated version of the war hammer was the maul. Primarily a domestic tool, mauls were wooden mallets used for a variety of purposes, but that also doubled as weapons of war when the poor of Europe were pressed into military service. So large and heavy was it that its wielder had little choice but to use both hands when using it. When taken into battle, mauls were often modified with the addition of reinforcing metal bands around the head, and metal spikes on its striking surface. Although comparatively primitive, this weapon could do truly appalling damage.

The mattock was an agricultural tool used for digging but, like the maul, was often used by the poor in battle. Looking somewhat like a pickax, a mattock was easy to lay one's hands on and was much less expensive than a sword.

The Ball and Chain

One of the weapons that is most closely associated with the knight is the ball and chain (or ball and chain mace, to give it its full name). Also called a *Morgenstern* (German for "morning star"), this was another gruesomely effective instrument, consisting of a heavy metal ball attached to a wooden handle by a two- to three-foot-long chain. (Occasionally warriors would use a variation on this with just the ball and chain, and no handle.) Its greatest use was against an opponent bearing a shield, for the ball — which was usually wickedly spiked — could be swung over, under, or around to strike. In the hands of a skillful wielder it could even be used to yank the shield away altogether, or to bring a man down from his horse. Needless to say, when swung around several times before striking, the speed and momentum of the ball could be increased enormously, and in such cases even plate armor could be pierced by a blow that was a combination of stabbing thrust and concussive impact.

Mace, Flail, and Lance

The mace was a more sophisticated version of the club, and consisted of a wooden handle with a metal weight attached to the end. During the medieval period, the wooden handle gave way to an all-metal construction, and these weapons were particularly effective at denting or even splitting armor and knocking an opponent senseless. In more peaceful times the scepter, a form of mace, came to symbolize power and legislative authority.

Similar to the mace — but bearing much more of a resemblance to the ball and chain — was the flail, which was composed of a wooden haft with multiple chains ending in spiked balls. This was a particularly potent weapon: a single flying ball was difficult enough to parry, but four or five were virtually impossible.

Finally we come to the weapon with which the medieval warrior is most closely identified: the lance. Basically a development of the primitive spear, the lance could be both thrust at an opponent and thrown over longer distances. The lance consisted of a long wooden shaft, to the end of which was attached either a spear head for battles or a narrow head for training and jousting. These heads were usually made of metal. The jousting lance was somewhat different from its battlefield counterpart, fanning out at the base, the center of gravity thus shifted toward the knight, who was required to hold it with one hand. They were made of wood with metal reinforcements at the breaking points, of which there were several. Metal jousting lances were unheard of, for two reasons: first, they would have been far too heavy to wield; and second, they needed to be able to break on contact, for jousts were not battles, and knights were not required to impale their opponents.

Body Armor

The knight's primary means of defense was his armor, and needless to say, there were many changes and innovations in these essential garments through the centuries. The primary mail garment was called a hauberk or birnie, and was a long shirt that fell well past the waist. An average hauberk might weigh about twenty pounds. Although they were extremely heavy, these garments were designed with mobility in mind. They were often slit up the front and back to allow the wearer to ride a horse, and they almost invariably had short, loose sleeves for greater ease in handling a sword. The knight's forearms would be protected by separate vambraces of mail or leather.

The word "hauberk" comes from the Old German *Halsberge,* meaning "coat of mail." Although they were first used in the eighth century, they were not very refined, and the garment referred to as a hauberk by modern historians was not commonly used until the early medieval period. The first hauberks were loose-fitting cloth jackets covered with bronze or iron scales. Later the sleeves would be extended to cover and protect the hands. The chain mail of which hauberks were made first appeared in the Bronze Age in Parthia and Scythia. Its versatility allowed it to be fashioned into a protective covering for any part of the knight's body, including gloves and footcoverings.

The traditional image of the knight completely encased in shining plate armor did not arise until the mid-1400s; prior to then armor was almost exclusively composed of chainmail or ringmail. It is likely that European mail was invented by the Celts several centuries before Christ. It was used by Roman warriors, Vikings, and Carolingian Paladins as well as by knights in the High Middle Ages. Unfortunately it is difficult to determine just how mail was manufactured, since although some of the armor has survived, the tools used to make it have not.

The process of making mail began with a sheet of metal hammered very thin and flat. The sheet would then be cut into narrow strips, and each strip would be wound around an iron mandrel or rod. (Later, when the technique of drawing wire was developed, soft iron wire would be used instead.) The wound strips would be sliced along the rod, possibly with a chisel or a saw, and the result of each cutting would be a handful of open rings.

To make mail, the armorer would join one ring to four or six others, and join each of these to four or six links, and so on, until he had a piece of metal fabric of the desired size. To keep the joined rings together, the armorer would rivet each link closed. This was done by first flattening the open ends of the ring, punching a hole in each flattened end, and then inserting a rivet through both holes. Mail of this type could be strengthened by including rings that had been punched from a sheet of metal rather than having been wound, cut, and closed.

The manufacture of this type of armor was extremely laborious, and consequently was too expensive for the average foot soldier. But for the knights who could afford it, it was a vital piece of equipment. Mail coverings were made for every part of the body, including arms, legs, feet, and hands. In fact, so versatile was mail that when plate armor began to see widespread use, mail was still used to protect a knight's shoulder, arm, and leg joints. Mail armor was immensely effective against bladed weapons: even the sharpest of swords could not easily slash through the thick mesh of metal links. However, blunt instruments such as clubs or maces could still crush flesh and bone, and it was a foolhardy knight who went into battle without adequate padding beneath his mail.

Although highly resistant to bladed weapons, mail could be pierced by a sharp implement directed against it with sufficient force. As weapons such as the longbow and the crossbow increased in power, mail armor became less and less useful. Crossbows were especially lethal, and prompted the Byzantine princess Anna Comnena to state, "not only can a crossbow bolt penetrate a buckler [shield], but a man and his armour, clean through." The longbow was also particularly fearsome; so much so that during the Hundred Years' War laws were passed in England requiring men to practice with it.

These developments in weapons technology resulted in the use of full plate armor, and there were as many styles as there were nations and monarchies in medieval Europe. It was, however, extremely expensive, and only knights and nobles could afford it. A knight in full plate armor, especially on horseback, was virtually impervious to attack with most weapons, until he was knocked down or off his horse. So heavy was the armor that when this happened, he was in serious trouble, and stood little chance against his opponents. A fallen knight would almost invariably become prey to any one of a number of terrifying weapons, such as the flanged mace, the military pick, or the war hammer, which was used to crack open the armor, revealing the defenseless body inside. Unless he received help very quickly, the fallen knight could expect to be stabbed, slashed or beaten to death. There were many different styles of full plate armor, the main distinctions being among those worn for mounted combat, dismounted combat, and jousting (see chapter 2).

Perhaps the most noticeable difference in jousting armor was that of the breastplate. Breastplates are probably the oldest form of armor, and there have been countless variations on the basic theme throughout history. Foot soldiers tended to favor lighter pieces that did not interfere with their mobility, while mounted warriors (for obvious reasons) were able to wear heavier pieces, affording them protection from spears and lances. For the joust, breastplates were developed featuring a central protrusion that would deflect the thrust of a lance. Another variation on the breastplate was known as the cuirass, which had the addition of a backplate and could be worn by itself, or as part of a complete suit of plate armor.

Finally there was the surcoat, which was not really armor, but rather the robe used to cover it. We tend to associate surcoats with the Crusader knight more than any other, and it is true that they first appeared in Europe during the Crusades. Although at first sight they might appear to offer no protection to the knight whatsoever, surcoats were actually a vitally important piece of his equipment. In the searing heat of the Middle East a coat of unprotected chain mail would heat up very quickly and might easily prove fatal; the surcoat prevented this. The garment was also extremely useful in rain-sodden northern Europe, protecting the mail from dampness and rust.

Usually made from cloth or wool, the surcoat was slit to waist level to allow the wearer to ride a horse comfortably, and was tied around at the waist with a belt or a cord. They were also decorated with heraldic symbols; for example, the Knights Templar wore a red cross upon their breasts (see chapter 7). Some historians believe that these symbols were the first examples of heraldry in Europe.

Helms

The knight's head and neck were protected by a mail coif or hood, and often he would wear a helm on top of the coif for added protection. At first helms were rather simple, conical affairs, with a nasal, a narrow strip of metal giving protection to the vulnerable nose. Over the years helms would evolve into more and more elaborate designs, such as the open-faced burgonet, developed in Burgundy in the sixteenth century and used chiefly by cavalry soldiers. Burgonets generally consisted of an upright, conical skull with a peak above the eyes, similar to a modern baseball cap, and hinged earpieces. Sometimes a panache, or plume holder, would be attached to the crown of the helmet. In fact, the phrase "to be crest-fallen" derives from a type of medieval tournament in which each contestant attempted to knock the crest off the other's helmet. The winner was the combatant left with his crest and helmet intact; the loser was "crestfallen."

Perhaps the helmet most closely associated with the typical "knight in shining armor" was the armet, which fully enclosed the face and the head. It was most popular in the fifteenth and sixteenth centuries, when European knights wore plate mail into battle. The armet consisted of a skull piece; hinged cheek pieces, which locked at the front; and a visor piece; together these pieces completely enclosed the knight's face. Armets have often been confused with close helmets, which had a full visor and a bevor (a chin and neck guard); the visor pivoted up and down on bolts attached to each side of the skull piece, whereas the hinged cheek pieces of the armet opened backward from the front of the face. As with the armet, there is a contemporary expression that has its origin with the close helmet: the phrase "shut your face" can be traced back to the entreaties of fifteenth-century knights to each other to stop talking, close the visors of their helms, and prepare for combat.

The great helm was first developed in the twelfth century, and is the helmet most closely associated with the Crusader knight. This incredibly tough piece of equipment, which must have presented a terrifying sight to the knight's enemies, was cylindrical in shape and, in its early form, flat-topped, later being surmounted by a shallow cone. So heavy was it — up to twenty-five pounds — that it required an internal leather harness to support it upon the knight's head. It featured narrow eye slits that were offset toward the sides, to reduce the risk of penetration by sword, dagger, or lance, and small breathing holes. Although it offered considerable protection against bladed weapons and missiles, its main drawbacks were poor visibility and poor ventilation.

The cabasset was an open-faced helmet whose low manu-facturing cost made it very popular with infantry and pike-men in the sixteenth and seventeenth centuries (see chapter 8). Its pear-shaped design with a small, pointed projection at the crown bore a striking similarity to another helmet, the morion, which first appeared in the sixteenth century and is most closely associated with the Spanish conquistadors.

Shields

There were many different types of shield available to the medieval warrior. The smallest and simplest was the buckler, which was used more to deflect an opponent's blows than to give full protection to the body. More in keeping with the popular view of medieval combat is the kite shield. Together with its close relative the tear shield (so named because of its teardrop shape), the kite shield was particularly favored by the Normans (it is often referred to as a Norman shield), and was used between the eleventh and fifteenth centuries. Usu-ally made of wood reinforced with metal, it also was a fa-vorite of mounted knights, who found that its shape provided perfect cover between the shoulder and the knee. Very simi-lar to the kite shield was the wood and metal heater, which was used from the twelfth to the eighteenth centuries. It was shorter than the kite shield, usually covering the body be-tween the shoulder and the waist.

The wall shield (or pavis) was designed to completely cover the user's body and was particularly favored by archers. The reason was simple enough: archers and crossbowmen were very vulnerable while reloading and aiming their weapons. Crossbowmen especially could find themselves in serious trouble while placing the weapon on the ground and pulling back the bowstring. Thus the pavis was developed, featuring a strut on the base that could be pulled out and that would support the shield while the crossbowman dealt with his weapon. Alternatively the shield could be held in position by a squire, in this case called a pavisor.

Finally the tower shield was similar in design to the pavis but was a little smaller, covering the body from shoulder to knee when held. Often this type of shield featured a deeply curved top, somewhat like a bell in shape, which would protect the user's head without restricting his vision to either side.

The Warhorse

As noted in the introduction, the single most enduring image of the medieval period is surely the mounted, armored knight: noble, battle-hardened, and courageous, sitting atop his powerful caparisoned warhorse, the magnificent animal snorting in anticipation of the next fight. It is the move to horseback that presents the most significant development in warfare from the end of the Roman Empire to medieval Western Europe. Although well-organized infantry still played a very important role (and could even defeat heavy cavalry on the battlefield), the period of the Middle Ages was, as the historian Andrew Ayton says, "an equestrian age of war."

Of course, mounted warriors were far from an exclusive feature of the West: the Magyars of the ninth and tenth centuries and the Mongols of the thirteenth were superbly accomplished horsemen. The Magyars were the dominant people of Hungary, but also lived in Romania, Ukraine, Slovakia, and Yugoslavia. In the past scholars believed that a common origin existed among the Magyars, Huns, Mongols, and Turks; however, modern research has refuted this claim. The Magyars were a nomadic people who migrated in about A.D. 460 from the Urals to the northern Caucasus, where they remained for about four hundred years. They seem to have maintained close contact with Turkic peoples, since many Magyar words are of Turkish origin (the Magyar or Hungarian language itself belongs to the Finno-Ugric family). In the late ninth century the Magyars were forced westward across southern Russia and into present-day Romania by the Pechenegs, another nomadic culture whose origin is uncertain and who themselves were pushed west in the late ninth century by the Khazars.

The Magyar leader Arpad defeated the Bulgar czar Simeon I, but Simeon enlisted the aid of the Pechenegs and managed to force the Magyars north into Hungary, where they permanently settled in about 895. Both highly disciplined and extremely brutal, the Magyars conquered Moravia and forced their way deep into Germany until they were stopped in 955 by the Holy Roman emperor Otto I.

The Mongols were traditionally a pastoral people, with herds of horses, cattle, camels, and sheep, and who lived in large felt-covered dwellings known as yurts. As with the Pechenegs, the origin of the Mongols is unclear, but scholars believe that many of the Huns who invaded Europe may have been Mongols. The various Mongol tribes were only loosely confederated and frequently fought among themselves, and it was not until the early thirteenth century that the Mongols became a powerful nation with the creation of the Mongol Empire by Genghis Khan. The organization of the empire, together with the administration of the army and the various codes of law, were brought together under the Yasa, or imperial code. Following the Mongol advance into both Europe and China, their Eurasian empire was divided into four khanates: the Great Khanate (China and East Asia), which, under Kublai Khan, became the Yüan Dynasty; the

Jagatai khanate (Turkistan); the Kipchack khanate (the Empire of the Golden Horde), founded by Batu Khan in Russia; and the Persian khanate.

These great warrior peoples were heavily dependent on the horse, as was the medieval West, with the *chevauchée* (a swift raid on horseback) a frequent battle tactic. Even when mounted fighting did not form part of the battle strategy (as with the English during the Hundred Years' War), horses were still immensely useful in terms of an army's mobility.

There were considerable differences, however, between warhorses and horse management of the East and those of the West. Unfortunately there is little we can say with absolute certainty regarding the medieval warhorse in the West. According to the historian Andrew Ayton:

> In the absence of direct documentary evidence or a substantial quantity of skeletal remains, estimates of warhorse size have been based upon scrutiny of iconographical evidence — with all the interpretative difficulties which that entails — and of such artefacts as horse-shoes, bits, and horse armour, backed up by indirect documentary evidence (for example, records of dimensions of horse-transport vessels) and practical field experimentation.

The image of the armor-clad knight on a massive steed is therefore open to considerable debate. As Ayton comments, the available evidence seems to indicate that the "typical" later medieval warhorse was fourteen to fifteen hands in height (one hand being equal to four inches). This is not particularly large, at least by modern standards, although there was some increase in size and weight between the eleventh and fourteenth centuries, mainly due to the increasing demands placed on the animal by armor.

Initially equine armor was not especially burdensome or sophisticated, taking the form of a mail trapper. From the mid-thirteenth century horse armor was also made of hardened leather or metal plates, which covered the head and the chest as well. When added to the knight's armor, this became a significant weight for the horse to carry, and one estimate has it that a late fourteenth-century warhorse would have had to carry at least a hundred pounds more than a horse of the Anglo-Norman period.

In the late thirteenth century programs were instituted in England and France to acquire and breed warhorses of a quality higher than had hitherto been available. Horses of particularly high quality were imported from Spain, Lombardy, and the Netherlands and distributed among the knights of the military elite by means of horse fairs and gifts. This resulted in the breeding of the "great horse," which was very strong and capable of extreme aggression. Eventually warhorses (in particular the destrier) reached a height of fifteen to sixteen hands. The powerful destrier, however, was actually ridden by very few knights, the general preference being for the courser, whose mobility suited it well for the *chevauchées.*

Perhaps the most far-reaching effect on the use of warhorses in Europe resulted from the Moorish conquest of Iberia. The Moors brought with them the Barb, the Turkmene, and the Arabian, and also took advantage of fine Spanish breeds such as the Andalusian. According to Ayton:

> The high reputation of Spanish horses endured into the later Medieval period: as Charles of Anjou so memorably remarked, "all the sense of Spain is in the heads of the horses." The Normans acquired Spanish horses, through gifts or involvement in the Reconquista, and bred from them in the favourable conditions of Normandy, with results which were celebrated with such verve in the Bayeux Tapestry.

The Turks were less than impressed by the horses that had previously been bred in western Europe. The sturdy mounts that carried heavily armored knights into battle could not compare with the Turkmene and Arab horses in terms of speed, maneuverability, intelligence, and endurance in hot climates. These differences were amply displayed in the battle tactics of the Crusades, which saw Western knights favoring the massed charge on their thirteen-hundred-pound horses against their enemies, who would frequently disperse with great speed on their own mounts, which weighed on average only about eight hundred pounds. When the Crusaders came to a halt on their now-exhausted horses, the Muslims would simply attack them with bows and arrows from a distance.

4

Love and War

Throughout history the life of the knight was characterized by the system of discipline and social interaction known as chivalry. The medieval warriors trained themselves daily in the arts of attack and defense, and this gave rise to the idea of absolute control of body, mind, and speech. The concept of discipline in social interaction arose from the knight's absolute obedience to his lord; in addition, civilians were not permitted to fight, and from this arose the idea of treating all other knights, whether one's enemies or friends, fairly and equally. Indeed, the concept of chivalry defines the very institution of knighthood.

The ethics of chivalry first appeared in France and Spain, and from there spread through the rest of Europe and into England. The principal virtues toward which the chivalrous knight aspired were piety, honor, courtesy, chastity, and loyalty. There were three claimants to his loyalty: God, his eternal master; his liege lord, who was his master while on Earth; and the mistress of his heart, the lady to whom he had sworn his love. In this sense the love he swore was often platonic, and was almost invariably pledged to a virgin, or to the wife of another man.

Chivalry assumed a religious dimension through the

participation of the church in the ceremonies of knighthood, although in earlier times it was taught that Christianity and the profession of arms were utterly incompatible. This change in the church's attitude probably arose from the Crusades, when Christian armies were for the first time devoted to a sacred purpose. And yet, even before the Crusades, the germ of this reconciliation can be found in the custom known as the Truce of God.

The Truce of God was a temporary suspension of hostilities, as distinct from the Peace of God, which was perpetual. The Truce of God dates from the eleventh century, and arose amid the anarchy of feudalism and the private wars that had made a battlefield of Europe. This truce had its origin in the Council of Elne in 1207, which sanctified Sunday and forbade all hostilities from Saturday night until Monday morning. Later this prohibition was extended to the days of the week consecrated by Christian mysteries: Thursday, in memory of the Ascension; Friday, the day of the Passion; and Saturday, the day before the Resurrection. Advent and Lent were also included in the truce. Thus were efforts made to limit the dreadful scourge of private war without suppressing it completely. The penalty for noncompliance was excommunication. The Truce of God soon spread from France to Italy and Germany. Although the problem of private war was not completely solved at one stroke, the impetus was nevertheless there. Gradually, the public authorities, royalty, and the leagues between nobles and the communes followed the orders of the church, and war became restricted to international conflicts.

It was then that the clergy saw its chance to extract from the violent warriors of feudal times a religious vow to use their weapons mainly in defense of the weak and helpless, especially women and orphans . . . and churches. The ideal of chivalry thus rested on a vow; and it was this vow that gave a religious dignity to the soldier, the man of war, elevating him in his own esteem, and raising him almost to the level of the monk in medieval society. In response, the church ordained a special blessing for the knight in a ceremony called *Benedictio novi militis*. From a very simple initial form, this ritual developed into an elaborate ceremony. To begin with, the aspirant was required to undertake confession, a prayer vigil, fasting, a symbolic bath, and investiture with a white robe, which represented the purity of soul required to embark upon the noble career of knight. Kneeling in the presence of the clergy, the knight-to-be pronounced the solemn vow of chivalry, whereupon the man chosen as godfather struck him lightly on the neck with the flat of a sword (the dubbing mentioned earlier) in the name of God and St. George, the patron saint of chivalry.

The practice of the chivalric code could, on occasion, border on the faintly ridiculous. Jim Bradbury offers this example:

> An unusual incident at Rennes, in 1356, demonstrated many of the perceived virtues: a besieging knight, John Bolton, boldly challenged his hungry enemies on the battlements, waving at them a bag of partridges; a besieged knight, Olivier de Mauny, came down to fight him, swimming the moat and winning the contest to claim the birds. Bolton was wounded in the fight, but Mauny out of respect for the good show he had put up, released him; Mauny, it was said, loved honor more than silver. Then Mauny became ill, and in respect for his opponent, and from a debt of honor, Bolton arranged for Mauny to receive a safe-conduct through the lines, and be treated by an English physician.

Bradbury goes on to cite several instances where the chivalric code was broken in no uncertain terms, such as at the siege of Rouen, when English prisoners were tied up with dogs in sacks and thrown into the Seine to drown. Indeed, decent treatment of prisoners was by no means guaranteed; and imprisonment for a ransom was often a fatal experience for the imprisoned. When a knight surrendered, he was considered to be under the protection of his captor and, until a ransom was paid, should under the rules of chivalry be allowed to lead as normal a life as the situation allowed. This did not always happen, however, as in the case of a knight called Henry Gentian, who was requested by his captor to agree to a larger ransom. When he refused his teeth were knocked out with a hammer. The earl of Worcester had a particularly unpleasant way of dealing with his prisoners, which was to impale them through the anus, surely as unequivocal a breach of the chivalric code as it is possible to imagine.

To attack one's enemies on the Sabbath was considered out of the question, and yet, as Bradbury comments:

> [T]he Sabbath truce was often broken, in order to make a surprise attack. At Liège the duke of Burgundy favoured such an attack, but was opposed by Louis XI, who however gave way. . . . The citizens were certainly not expecting an attack, and had gone for their Sunday dinner: "in every house we found the table set." In the same attack, Burgundy killed one of his own men for robbing a church! No wonder we sometimes find it hard to fathom the medieval mind.

Mercenaries gradually came to replace the mounted knight as the principal element in medieval armies; and yet mercenaries, too, often followed the chivalric code, mainly because many of them were themselves knights. Sir John Hawkwood (see chapter 8) is a case in point; for although he sold his martial talents to the highest bidder, he nevertheless believed that an honorable man should display loyalty and other virtues, in particular the protection of women. So highly regarded was he that when he was captured, his employers considered him well worth the ransom that was demanded for his safe return.

On one occasion his employer, Cardinal Robert of Geneva, ordered a less than enthusiastic Hawkwood to act without mercy against the inhabitants of the town of Cesena. Hawkwood followed his orders, but saved a thousand women by sending them to Rimini. As Bradbury reminds us, the problem for the mercenary was that he earned his living by war; in peacetime he would find himself out of a job, and garrison service was not particularly well paid. In Hawkwood's own words: "I live by war, and peace would be my undoing."

For those breaking the chivalric code, there were definite penalties. Cowardice, for instance, was especially frowned upon, and those guilty of it could expect to be stripped of their knighthood in consequence. Punishment could be even more severe, as in the case of the count of Dammertin, who was hanged in his armor as a result of cowardice.

There were also times when persuasion could work wonders with an otherwise merciless victor who was prepared to ignore the code. During the Hundred Years' War between England and France, Edward III was such a victor. When he captured the northern French port of Calais, Edward fully intended to kill everyone in the town. The chronicler Froissart describes the encounter in which the king changed his mind, and offered mercy instead of the sword.

When Sir Walter [de Manny] presented the men of Calais to him, the King glowered at them in silence for he hated the inhabitants of Calais bitterly, for all the harm and trouble they had caused him at sea.

The six burghers knelt before the King and, joining their hands together, threw themselves on his mercy. The King remained speechless with anger for a time, and when he spoke it was to give orders for them to be beheaded. All the knights and barons present begged the King as earnestly as they could to show them mercy. But he would not listen to them.

Then Sir Walter de Manny spoke up and said: "Ah, sir, please restrain your anger. You have a reputation for great nobility of soul. Do not therefore destroy it by an action of this kind, and give people cause to defame you. If you do not take pity on these men, but put them to death, the whole world will regard it as great cruelty. Of their own free will, these men have put themselves at your mercy to save their fellow citizens."

The King replied in anger: "Sir Walter, they will be beheaded. The people of Calais have caused the death of so many of my men that they too must die."

The Queen of England, whose pregnancy was far advanced, then fell on her knees, and with tears in her eyes implored him: "Ah! my lord, since I have crossed the sea in great danger, I have never asked you any favour. But now I humbly beg you, for the Son of the Blessed Mary and for the love of me, to have mercy on these six men!"

The King looked at her for some minutes without speaking, and then said: "Ah, lady, I wish you were anywhere else but here. You have entreated me in such a way that I cannot refuse. Therefore, though I do it with great reluctance, I hand them over to you. Do as you like with them."

The Queen thanked him from the bottom of her heart, and had the halters removed from their necks. She took them to her rooms, had them clothed and gave them a good dinner. She then gave them six nobles each, and had them escorted safely out of the camp.

While this was undoubtedly a merciful act, Bradbury reminds us that Edward was almost certainly making "a dramatic propaganda show of his mercifulness."

The history of chivalry can be divided into four distinct periods, following the period of foundation during which the Truce of God was in force and which succeeded, at least partially, in curbing the feudal savagery of the age. The first period was that of the Crusades, the golden age of chivalry, and the Crusader was seen as the very essence of the perfect knight. In return for the rescue of Palestine's holy places from Muslim domination and the defense of the pilgrims traveling there, the Crusader knights received the church's special protection in the form of the remission of all penances, dispensation from the jurisdiction of the secular courts, and the granting of a tenth of all church revenues to defray the expenses of traveling to the Holy Land.

The second period of chivalry was that of the military orders, the need for which arose following the conquest of Jerusalem and the importance of defending the Holy City from the attentions of the surrounding hostile nations. The three most important of these orders were the Sovereign Military Order of Malta, the Knights Templar, and the Teutonic Knights. In these orders the perfect fusion of the military and religious spirit was realized, and was represented most notably by such Crusaders as Godfrey of Bouillon, Tancred of Normandy, Richard Coeur de Lion, and Louis IX of France. The knightly vow bound with common ties warriors from every nation, enrolling them in a vast brotherhood with the same manners, ideals, and aims. Among the rules observed by this brotherhood were fidelity to their lords and to their word, fairness on the battlefield, and the strict observance of honor and courtesy. In addition, medieval chivalry inspired an entirely new movement in European literature, reflecting the ideal of knighthood and celebrating its achievements.

The third period, secular chivalry, arose following the Crusades. Knights continued to place great emphasis on honor, and this emphasis is displayed in the many knightly exploits of the Hundred Years' War. This turbulent period was filled with a heady mixture of bloody battles, tournaments, and gorgeous pageants. England had her heroes, such as the Black Prince, Chandos, and Talbot; France had Du Guesclin, Boucicaut, and Dunois. It was at this stage that the concept of courtly love took hold, and there arose a new type of knight: the chevalier devoted to the service of a noble lady. The courtly knight would worship this idol of his heart — who might very well be another man's wife — at a distance, and on many occasions these infatuations led to unfortunate results.

This philosophy of love and code of lovemaking is a curious concept that many of us in the twenty-first century find somewhat bemusing. The ultimate origin of courtly love is obscure, but probably derived from the works of Ovid and the songs of the troubadours, the lyric poets of the twelfth and thirteenth centuries who were attached to the courts of Provence and northern Italy, and who composed songs in complex metrical forms.

According to the procedure of courtly love, a man was supposed to fall hopelessly and passionately in love with a married woman of equal or higher social rank. He was required to suffer his love in silence for several months before declaring his passionate devotion. The lady in question would then reject his advances, claiming that her virtue would not allow such a thing. This would be followed by renewed wooing on the part of the love-crippled knight, who would swear his eternal and undying loyalty to her, and frequently claim that death from a broken heart was rapidly approaching. He would then attempt to prove his devotion by embarking on all manner of courageous exploits, which often amounted to taking part in tournaments (see chapter 2) and showing off his equestrian and jousting skills to the object of his passion.

When all this had been done, the lovers pledged themselves to each other in secrecy, vowing to remain faithful no matter what should befall them. Often following the knight's victory at a tournament, the lady would finally surrender herself to him, and their secret love would be consummated. The relationship would then enter a new phase, in which the knight and his lover embarked on various adventures and subterfuges, all with the purpose of avoiding detection by the husband.

Courtly love was of most significance as a literary device, and it features in many works of the period, such as Chrétien de Troyes's *Lancelot* of the twelfth century, Guillaume de Lorris's *Roman de la Rose* of the thirteenth century, and Chaucer's *Troilus and Criseyde* of the fourteenth. Like other aspects of chivalry, which were in reality frequently undermined by the corruption of their practitioners, courtly love eventually degenerated into an excuse for promiscuity.

In its final stage chivalry was reduced merely to a court service. The Order of the Garter, founded in 1348 by Edward III, and the Order of the Golden Fleece of Philip of Burgundy, dating from 1430, formed a brotherhood, not of battle-hardened Crusaders, but of courtiers. Their aim was little more than to contribute to the self-conscious splendor of their sovereign. Their activities were confined to nothing more serious than tournaments and jousts, and they made their vows not in chapels but in banqueting halls. One of the most celebrated of these vows was the "vow of the pheasant," made in 1454 at the court of Philip of Burgundy. Although the motive was of the utmost importance, being nothing less than the rescue of Constantinople, which had fallen to the Turks the previous year, the vow itself was taken under the most frivolous of circumstances, before God and the pheasant at a sumptuous banquet. The money that was poured into this affair might indeed have been better spent on the expedition itself, and although no fewer than 150 knights took the vow, the great undertaking came to nothing; all that was really considered to be of importance was the empty promise. Under these circumstances it is hardly surprising that the literature of the period came to hold chivalry in contempt, a contempt that found its most striking and famous expression in Cervantes's fabulous work *Don*

Quixote. In addition, and certainly more importantly, heavy cavalry was being made obsolete on the battlefield by the increasing use of infantry. Finally, with the advent of gunpowder and the general use of firearms in battle, chivalry disappeared altogether.

5

Castles and Siegecraft

Before and after Rome

If the mounted, armored warrior can be seen as the most potent and resonant symbol of the medieval era, an equally important and romantic image must be that of the castle, perhaps the greatest architectural and technological achievement of the period. Indeed, its importance in medieval society, in times of both peace and war, cannot be overestimated. Today the landscape of Europe and the Middle East is dotted with the remains — in varying states of repair — of these magnificent constructions, their titanic masonry carrying the echoes of bloody battles long past.

Although the most enduring image associated with the castle is that of the besieged band of knights hiding behind massive stone walls while the enemy launched vicious assaults upon them, this is far from being its main function. As Philip Warner states, the main function of the castle was not to retreat from conflict but to control it. Before we examine the various forms and developments in castle-building technology over the centuries, we must first return to the years before the Roman Empire, where we shall discover the seeds that would give rise to these massive fortifications.

The architects of pre-Roman fortifications did not build edifices upon the landscape as such, but rather modified the landscape itself, creating gigantic ditches and embankments with the simplest of tools. Among the most famous of these ancient sites in England are the Iron Age fortress of White Horse Hill in the county of Berkshire, in the central south of the country; and the concentric fortress of Old Sarum in Wiltshire, to the west. The outer ring of Old Sarum was constructed at an unknown date, now perhaps irretrievably lost beyond the horizon of time. However, following the invasion of 1066, the Normans built a castle inside the three-hundred-foot-diameter central ring, which is now no more than a centuries-battered ruin. Among the most awe-inspiring of these ancient edifices is the four-thousand-year-old Maiden Castle in Dorset, which lies to the far southwest in England. On many occasions, when fire was employed as a weapon during attacks, the stone and timber of which the walls were composed became fused into a single substance. The ramparts of these so-called vitrified fortresses are of colossal strength.

Roman military strategy did not place great emphasis on fixed defensive fortifications, preferring to rely on the obvious advantages of highly trained and mobile forces that could utilize the potential defensive features in the field of battle. That is not to say, of course, that Rome itself was not adequately fortified; on the contrary, as Philip Warner reminds us, the wall that surrounded the city was twelve miles long and twelve feet thick, with a height of sixty feet along most of its length and with siege towers every hundred feet.

Likewise, in their conquered lands the Romans accepted the need for fortified defenses at certain places, most notably along the southeastern coast of England, which was vulnerable to incursions by the Saxons. Once again, the Normans took advantage of earlier remains, and just as they had done at Old Sarum, they added castles to the Roman wall at Pevensey in the county of Sussex, and at Portchester in Hampshire.

The Romans protected their garrisons well; this can be seen

especially in London, whose walls enclosed some 330 acres but whose gateways are long demolished, their foundations mere architectural echoes of their former presence. Northeast of London lies the town of Colchester, one of the great settlements of pre-Roman Britain and the capital of the leader Cunobelin (the model for Shakespeare's Cymbeline). Colchester was a very important Roman garrison and thus was more than adequately protected, with walls eight feet thick, in addition to a twenty-foot-wide rampart. If anything, Colchester was overfortified, and the reason for this is very clear, being the result of one of the most tragic and legendary events of the Roman occupation of Britain. Boadicea — also (and properly) called Boudicca — was queen of the Iceni tribe of East Anglia. Her husband, King Prasutagus, died in about A.D. 60, dividing his property equally between the Roman emperor and his daughters. However, the Romans, in an act of great brutality and stupidity, seized the entire Iceni kingdom. Beaten with rods and her daughters raped, Boudicca vowed vengeance. She drew together a coalition of tribes and led the Iceni against their persecutors, sacking Colchester, together with London and the town of Verulamium (which is now St. Albans, Hertfordshire).

At the time (A.D. 61) the Roman governor of Britain, Caius Suetonius Paulinus, who had previously served in Mauretania under Emperor Claudius I, was focusing his attention on a campaign against the Druid stronghold of Mona on the island of Anglesey off the coast of North Wales. With the Ninth Legion routed and the important garrison town of Colchester plundered and in flames, Paulinus was recalled to southern Britain to suppress the Iceni revolt, which he did with horrible efficiency. Her armies defeated, Boudicca herself committed suicide by poison the same year.

In the declining years of the empire, it became less and less feasible to engage enemies on the field of battle; and as a consequence the idea of physical defenses grew in importance in the minds of military strategists. So work began on the truly colossal project of constructing walls to enclose the empire itself. These walls, or *limes*, were intended to hold back an invading force long enough for reinforcements to be brought in. Warner cites the Limes Germanicus as a good example of this type of fortification. This enormous earthwork, extending from the Rhine between Bonn and Coblenz to Abusina on the Danube, took the form of an embankment topped with a palisade and punctuated with watchtowers. As would castle builders of later centuries, the builders of the Limes Germanicus took full advantage of the land upon which the structure was built, making use of natural features such as mountains and rivers, enlisting the aid of nature's own creations to obstruct the advance of aggressors.

Impressive as the earthwork was, for Emperor Hadrian (who ruled from A.D. 117 to 138), the Limes Germanicus was far from satisfactory. He had it rebuilt with stone, on a straighter course, and such a powerful symbol of might did it become that it came to be known as "the Wall of the Devil."

Hadrian was born in Spain in A.D. 76; his full name was Publius Aelius Hadrianus. He demonstrated a great talent both as a warrior (serving as a commander in Dacia) and as an administrator. An orphan, he had been the ward of the Emperor Trajan, who chose him to be his successor upon his death. His reign was as efficient and vigorous as had been his previous career, although he abandoned Trajan's aggressive policy in Asia. However, Hadrian could also be quite ruthless, as his attitude to the Jews in the Holy Land makes clear.

Initially Hadrian was sympathetic to the Jews, allowing them to return to Jerusalem and granting permission for the rebuilding of their Holy Temple. He later reneged on his promise and decided that the site of the Temple should be moved. In response to this betrayal the Jews began to organize guerrilla forces and, in 123, began to launch surprise attacks on Roman targets. Hadrian's response was to send an extra legion, the Sixth Ferrata, into Judea to deal with the situation. In 132, Hadrian began to establish a city called

Aelia Capitolina and began work on a temple to the Roman god Jupiter Capitolinus. When Hadrian left Judea that year, the Jewish rebellion began in earnest. Under the leadership of the charismatic Shimon Bar-Kochba, the Jews captured some fifty strongholds in Palestine and nearly a thousand towns and villages, including Jerusalem.

These successes could not last, however, and the turning point came when Hadrian sent general Julius Severus from Britain, along with Hadrianus Quintus Lollius Urbicus, who had previously been governor of Germania. Severus chose a combination of siege and sudden attack against the Jewish rebels, at first starving the settlements and then storming and demolishing them. Bar-Kochba's headquarters were in the town of Bethar, which also contained the Sanhedrin, the Jewish High Court. Bethar was also of extreme strategic importance due to its location overlooking the Sorek Valley and the Jerusalem–Bet Guvrin Road. In addition, thousands of refugees had sought safety in Bethar during the war. In 135 Hadrian laid siege to the town, and on the 9th of Av, the day on which the Jews commemorated the destruction of the first and second Holy Temples, Bethar fell. Once inside the town, the Romans massacred everyone. In the aftermath of Bethar, the Jews were sold into slavery and forbidden to live in Jerusalem, which Hadrian renamed Colonia Aelia Capitolina. The persecution of the Jews continued for the rest of Hadrian's reign.

Of course, now Hadrian is most famous for the wall that bears his name, between England and Scotland. Hadrian's Wall extended for some seventy-three miles between Solway Firth and Tynemouth. For the majority of its length it was more than seven feet thick and stood fifteen feet high, with fortresses every four miles. Like the Limes Germanicus, it took advantage of hilly regions, while along stretches of flat ground it was made more secure by deep ditches in front. An additional wall was built between the Forth and the Clyde after Scotland had been partially conquered, during the reign of Hadrian's successor Antoninus. The Antonine Wall was smaller, but the fact that its fortresses were more closely spaced meant that it was no less secure.

The Saxons arrived in England during the Roman occupation, prompting the construction of a number of castles in the southeast, such as Pevensey and Caister. A Germanic people first mentioned by Ptolemy as inhabiting the southern part of Jutland, the Saxons gradually extended their presence from the mouth of the Elbe River southward, across the Weser River. Brave, resourceful, and ruthless, the Saxons were ruled by princes and chieftains, who consulted with representatives of all levels of their society (with the exception of slaves) on all issues. In the third and fourth centuries A.D., they raided the coasts of the North Sea, and were only too well known to the Romans, who named the European coast from the Loire to the Scheldt Rivers Litora Saxonica, or Saxon shores. By the fifth century, which saw the final phase of the Roman occupation of Britain, the Saxons increased their attacks on the southern coast, and also began to settle there. Their method of arrival in Britain notwithstanding, relations between the Saxons and the Romans were more cordial than one might have supposed, and the Romans even came to regard them as suitable heirs to their British territories.

When the Romans finally left, in 410, the Britons were left with fortifications and a superb system of roads, but lacked the manpower or the training to make proper use of them, and so once again England was invaded by forces who made good use of the roads to penetrate far into the country. From the north came the Picts and the Scots; from the south, the Angles, Jutes and Saxons. Warner informs us that the "Saxons referred to their opponents as 'Waelisch,' which meant foreigners. The Waelisch were driven to Cornwall, to Brittany (in France) and into what is now called Wales."

It was not long before British shores witnessed the catastrophic arrival of yet another invader, one whose name has become synonymous with violent conquest: the Vikings.

They first raided England in 787, landing in Dorset in the southwest of the country, beginning an era that would become drenched with blood and terror. The origin of the word "Viking" is unclear, and may come from *wicing* (warrior) or from *wic*, the waterways they utilized to take them inland. These Scandinavian raiders were extremely ruthless, and Europe trembled whenever their longboats were sighted. Their way of life was characterized by *berserkgangr*, meaning "joy in battle," and it is a characteristic that, as more than one historian has noted, came to greatly influence life in the medieval period.

Normandy suffered much from Viking assaults, until Rollo of Normandy (c. 860–c. 932) signed the Treaty of Saint-Clair-sur-Epte with Charles the Simple, king of the Franks, in 911. By this treaty, Rollo received the territory around Rouen that his men had occupied, on the condition that he defend it against invasion and that he be baptized. According to Philip Warner in *The Medieval Castle:*

> Rollo appears to be one of those people who leave a lasting mark on history but are themselves almost unknown. Legend has it that he may have been Rolf the Ganger, an exiled Norwegian who had, perhaps to escape someone's vengeance, moved first to Scotland, then Ireland, and finally France. It has been said that he was too heavy (or too tall) for a small Norwegian horse to carry, and this gave him his name of "the walker"; it seems more likely that he was a "goer, a wanderer." The word "gang" became widely known when Robert Burns, in the eighteenth century, wrote
> > "The best laid schemes of mice and men
> > Gang aft agley."
> and keeps its original meaning in "gangplank."

The treaty Rollo signed with Charles gave Rollo considerable possessions in Normandy, and these territories were

added to after his death in 933 by his son, William Longsword. William was murdered by the duke of Flanders in 942
and left his properties to a boy named Richard, who died in
996. His successor was a pious and just man, also named
Richard, who became known as Richard the Good, and was
followed by yet another Richard. This one was rather unfortunate, falling victim to poison given to him by his own
brother only a year after he claimed his inheritance. The poi-
soner was named Robert, and seems to have aroused feelings
of both extreme admiration and enmity in those around him,
for he was known not only by the name Robert the Magnificent, but also was identified by some with the legendary
Robert the Devil, a mysterious figure who was said to have
been sold by his mother to the Devil before his birth. Upon
discovering this, he did much penance and was ultimately
able to purify himself. There are both French and English
versions of the story, which was the inspiration for Meyer-
beer's opera *Robert le Diable*. Robert was out near Falaise in
Normandy one day when his attention fell on a tanner's
daughter named Arlette, who was washing clothes in a
stream. The product of his fancy was a boy who later was
known as William the Bastard . . . and also as William the
Conqueror and William I, king of England.

William succeeded to the Norman dukedom upon his father's death while on a pilgrimage to Jerusalem in 1035.
William is believed to have visited England in about 1051, and
there received a promise from his cousin Edward the Confessor that he would become king upon Edward's death. In
1053 he married Matilda, daughter of Baldwin, count of Flanders, despite being forbidden to do so by the pope. The increased prestige that came with this union, combined with
William's growing power, brought conflict with King Henry
of France, although the accession of Philip I (whose guardian was William's father-in-law) alleviated these problems
somewhat. Soon after William conquered Maine in 1063, he
had a piece of good fortune with the wrecking of the ship of

Harold Godwinson, earl of Wessex, on the French coast. Harold was taken to William and, in return for his release, promised to support William's interests in England.

However, Harold was crowned king of England in 1066, and upon hearing of this, William raised a fleet and an army, sailed for England, and killed Harold at the Battle of Hastings that same year. Following this battle, resistance was slight, and offered little impediment to William's taking of London, where he was crowned king on Christmas Day. Although many of the nobility had been slain at Hastings, many survived, and in the hope of maintaining a continuity of rule, William allowed them to keep their lands and possessions. In spite of this a series of rebellions by the English occurred, which William lost no time in suppressing with ruthless force. Now the lands of the nobility were taken and redistributed to William's Norman followers according to the rules of feudalism (described in chapter 1). He later undertook reform of the church, taking control of church affairs and substituting foreign prelates for many English bishops. In 1085 he ordered a survey of England to be taken, and the result was one of the most famous documents in English history, the Domesday Book. In 1087 he was fatally injured in a riding accident, and died at Rouen.

Anglo-Saxon Fortifications

Before journeying into the heyday of the medieval castle, it is worthwhile to pause briefly to examine another precursor of those titanic buildings that so greatly influenced the landscape and history of the period. While castles were being constructed in the East, West European tribes such as the Anglo-Saxons developed a far more primitive type of fortification known as a burh. They were really little more than refuges that warriors could use in emergencies, and were composed of timber palisades and deep ditches. Although few burhs have survived (most were subsequently built over and became towns with names ending in "bury" or "burgh"), Warner offers us the example of Witham in the southeastern county of Essex, which possesses the remains of a burh enclosing an area of twenty-six acres, with several mounds and ditches.

Aside from form and construction, there is one essential difference between the burh and the castle that would supersede it: burhs were constructed by the community for the community's benefit and protection, whereas the castle was to protect only the knight and his family. In spite of the preponderance of burhs at the time there is documentary evidence that private castles and forts did exist: in 864 Charles the Bald, king of the Franks, issued a decree that all such buildings should immediately be demolished.

The Motte and Bailey Castle

Although they differed from each other considerably in their design, motte and bailey castles possessed the same fundamental characteristics. The main feature was the motte (from the Norman word for turf), an enormous mound of earth with very steep sides that could not be negotiated by a mounted warrior, surrounded by a deep ditch. This ditch could either be filled with water (the word "motte" would become "moat" and be used to describe a water-filled ditch), or it could be filled with wooden stakes and other dangerous objects. This mound was usually fifty to one hundred feet high, and could be up to three hundred feet across at the flattened top. The top was enclosed with a wall of timber logs, the palisade, and the area inside this wall would contain the tower or donjon, a one- or two-story-high structure originally constructed of wood. Around the water- or stake-filled ditch was another wall, and the area within was known as the bailey, or keep.

The word "donjon" did not originally carry the connotations of imprisonment and suffering that it does today. Its derivation is from Low Latin and means "dominating point." It was only after the arrival of stone castles, containing more luxurious (at least in medieval terms) comforts, that the donjons began to be used to house prisoners.

Historians generally accept that the earliest known castles in Europe stood in the same region of the Loire Valley in France: Doué-la-Fontaine and Langeais. Doué has an interesting history, one that Jim Bradbury summarizes in his excellent study *The Medieval Siege*. This Carolingian palace was built in about 900 by the count of Blois, but was partially destroyed by fire. It was restored in the mid-tenth century, and an extra story was added. During this reconstruction project the ground-floor entrance was blocked, leaving ingress only by the first floor. In about 1000, a motte was added. Some historians argue that then Doué ceased to be merely a residence and became a castle. However, it was not long before "Europe's first castle" fell: in about 1025 it was captured by Fulk Nerra, count of Anjou. With regard to the origin of European castles, Bradbury makes the point that "the emergence of 'castles' was in most cases simply the improvement of the defences of existing defended residences. Purpose built castles would emerge, but many of our best known early castles were existing residences, usually already defended."

He goes on to suggest that one possible cause of the development of motte and bailey castles was the necessity of building on higher ground to avoid the flooding that frequently occurred in low-lying coastal regions. This design may well have been retained in areas where flooding was not a problem simply because it offered an excellent defense not only against the elements but also against other human beings.

These castles could vary widely in size and shape, and many had more than one bailey. Although their construction was a straightforward affair, they were incredibly resilient structures, and it was no mean feat to conquer one. They are most closely associated with the Norman conquerors, who built hundreds across England after the Conquest of 1066.

A particularly valuable source of information on Norman castles is the Bayeux Tapestry (which actually is not a tapestry at all but an embroidery of colored wool on an unbleached linen background). It is composed of a series of pictorial panels 203 feet in length and approximately 18 inches high. As with many important documents that have come down through many centuries, the Bayeux Tapestry is shrouded in obscurity. It was probably made about ten years after the Conquest, most likely by English embroiderers at Winchester. Historians largely agree that it was commissioned by Odo, bishop of Bayeux and William the Conqueror's half brother, and was finished in time for the consecration of the cathedral at Bayeux. It has been suggested by some that the tapestry was hung around the nave of the cathedral on feast days, although this seems unlikely, since it is not long enough.

It was nearly ruined during the French Revolution, when it was used to cover a wagonload of ammunition bound for the northern front. A lawyer from Bayeux saw this and immediately replaced the priceless tapestry with a waterproof cloth, taking the tapestry home and placing it in his attic for safekeeping. It remained there for the next three decades, before being retrieved and placed in the palace of the bishop of Bayeux.

The first half of the tapestry tells the story of Harold Godwinson, who, as we saw earlier in this chapter, was shipwrecked on the French coast and ransomed from the count of Ponthieu by William the Bastard, who secured Harold's promise to support his interests in England. The second half chronicles William's preparations for the invasion of England and the Battle of Hastings. Of most interest to us, however, is the tapestry's depiction of castles, particularly those of

Rennes and Dinan, and the construction of the motte at Hastings. Interestingly one can see quite clearly horizontal bands within the motte, which was puzzling to historians until archaeological excavations showed that mottes were often constructed of discrete layers of different materials bonded together to provide additional structural strength. The wooden tower standing atop the motte was shipped from Normandy in special prefabricated sections.

To the left of the motte and tower is a quite humorous depiction of a fight breaking out between two workmen, who are clubbing each other over the head with spades. This altercation is happening behind the overseer's back. This would seem a rather curious image to include; however, Warner reminds us that the labor force was made up of more than one conquered tribe, and that enmity toward each other probably outweighed that felt toward the Normans.

Warner goes on to quote the words of Lambert d'Ardres, who left a detailed description of a very elaborate wooden castle built in 1117 by Arnold, the seneschal (a steward in a medieval household) of the count of Boulogne:

Arnold, lord of Ardres, built on the motte of Ardres a wooden house, excelling all the houses of Flanders of that period both in material and in carpenter's work. The first storey was on the surface of the ground, where were cellars and granaries, and great boxes, tuns, casks, and other domestic utensils. In the storey above were the dwelling and common living rooms of the residents, in which were the larders, the rooms of the bakers and butlers, and the great chamber in which the lord and his wife slept. Adjoining this was a private room, the dormitory of the waiting maids and children. In the inner part of the great chamber was a certain private room, where at early dawn or in the evening or during sickness or at time of blood-letting, or for warming the maids and weaned children, they used to have a fire.

In the upper story of the house were garret rooms, in which on the one side the sons (when they wished it) on the other side the daughters (because they were obliged) of the lord of the house used to sleep. In this storey also the watchmen and the servants appointed to keep the house took their sleep at some time or other. High up on the east side of the house, in a convenient place, was the chapel, which was made like unto the tabernacle of Solomon in its ceiling and painting. There were stairs and passages from storey to storey, from the house into the kitchen, from room to room, and again from the house into the loggia, where they used to sit in conversation for recreation, and again from the loggia into the oratory.

The castle built at Montargis in 1056 sounds similarly elaborate, with a great hall in the upper story of the wooden tower. The majority of motte and bailey castles were rather simpler than this, however, with the bottom, middle, and upper stories housing the storeroom, the soldiers, and the lord and his family, respectively.

As might be expected, the decision where to site a castle was an enormously important one, given their nature and purpose. A poorly sited castle would not do its builders much good as a means of guarding roads and valleys, holding ground won in battle, acting as storage for materials, or as rest and recuperation facilities for battle-weary soldiers.

Food and Drink in a Medieval Castle

One of the features of these castles that would seem most odd to the citizen of a modern industrialized country was the open-air kitchen. There were very good reasons for this: first, to prevent the smells and smoke of cooking from filling the entire place; and second, to minimize the risk of accidental fires. The enjoyment of a well-prepared meal is, of course, something with which most of us can identify. For the medieval castle dweller, however, it was an event of truly epic proportions, and the typical banquet included dishes of such a range and quantity as would make the modern diner break out in a cold sweat.

To give a full account of the preparation and consumption of food in the medieval period would require a book in itself, and so we must content ourselves with a brief overview of this fascinating aspect of life in that far-off time. The health-conscious vegetarians of today would find themselves somewhat at a loss at a medieval banquet; and even the hardened meat-lover would find much that was strange to the eye and palate.

As might be expected, a lord would hold a banquet to impress his guests with his wealth and generosity. In 1575, for instance, Robert Dudley held a banquet that lasted for 19 days in honor of Queen Elizabeth, at which no fewer than 10 oxen were eaten every day. When Archbishop Neville was installed at York in 1467, a truly monumental feast was celebrated by 6,000 guests. This might seem a large number until we consider what was prepared for them. There were 104 oxen, six wild bulls, 1,000 sheep, 304 calves, 400 swans, 2,000 geese, 1,000 capons, 2,000 pigs, 104 peacocks, more than 13,000 other birds, 500 stags, 1,500 assorted pies, more than 600 pikes and breams, 12 porpoises and seals, and 13,000 assorted desserts, including jellies, tarts, and custards.

Of course, in the absence of modern conveniences such as freezers and refrigerators, the preservation of foodstuffs called for particular ingenuity and inventiveness. Where meat was concerned, the simplest method of preservation was to keep the animal alive for as long as possible. Otherwise, salting and smoking were the favored methods. Salting was performed in two ways: dry-salting was performed by pounding salt to a fine powder with a mortar and pestle and then covering the meat with it; brine-curing entailed immersing the meat in a strong salt solution. The salted meat would be thoroughly soaked and rinsed prior to cooking.

While meat was very often roasted and stewed, there were other methods of preparation that would doubtless strike many in the modern world as bizarre and unpalatable. Joseph Gies, in his fascinating book *Life in a Medieval Castle,* describes many of the items on offer. One such dish was blankmanger, which bears little resemblance to the popular British milk dessert blancmange. The medieval dish was similar to a custard — at least in consistency — but was made from chicken pounded to a paste and blended with rice boiled in almond milk, seasoned with sugar, and garnished with fried almonds and anise. Mortrews was a dish of dumplings made with meat or fish that was pounded, mixed with breadcrumbs and eggs, and then poached.

Bake mete was a pie in which meat or fish was baked with fruit and spices. Interestingly the word "mete" does not mean "meat," but rather "meal"; and such was the amount of ingredients in these pies that they were literally meals in themselves. As with the pastries that would be eaten by Cornish miners several centuries later, the pastry in which these pies were cooked was nothing more than a receptacle for the ingredients, and was not eaten. Brawen was the flesh of the wild boar, or "tusked swine." The word is of Germanic origin and is related to the Old English word *braed,* meaning flesh.

Birds were very popular at the medieval table, and the diners were not particularly concerned about size. The smaller birds used in cooking, such as swallows, hummingbirds, larks, and turtledoves were collectively called bryddes. Small birds were frequently used to stuff larger birds or other animals to make incredibly elaborate and heavy roast dishes.

Sauces were as popular then as they are today, and made liberal use of the herbs growing in the castle garden, together with vinegar, ginger, pepper, onions, saffron, and cloves, along with verjuice, or the juice from unripe grapes.

Fish also was very popular, and like meat would be smoked or salted before being rinsed and prepared with a variety of rich sauces. According to Gies: "Fresh herring, flavored with ginger, pepper, and cinnamon, might be made into a pie. Other popular fish included mullet, shad, sole, flounder, plaice, ray, mackerel, salmon, and trout. Sturgeon, whale, and porpoise were rare seafood delicacies, the first two 'royal fish,' fit for kings and queens. Pike, crab, crayfish, oysters, and eels were also favourites."

While the rich partook of these choice items, the poor had to be satisfied with staples such as peas and beans, which would be a mere accompaniment on an affluent dinner table. In addition, there was honey and fruits such as apples and peaches, as well as imported delicacies such as figs, oranges, and pomegranates. Sugar usually was sold in hard loaves, which were then pounded into powder. Gies describes the dining arrangements thus:

> The most important guests were at the high table, with the loftiest place reserved for an ecclesiastical dignitary, the second for the ranking layman. After grace, the procession of servants bearing food began. First came the pantler with the bread and butter, followed by the butler and his assistants with the wine and beer. Wine, in thirteenth-century England mostly imported from English-ruled Bordeaux, was drunk young in the absence of an effective technique for stoppering containers. Wine kept a year became undrinkable. No attention was paid to vintage, and often what was served even at rich tables was of poor quality.

One very popular type of wine was known as clarree (not to be confused with claret), which was flavored with honey, cinnamon, galingale, and pepper.

Etiquette was extremely important at the table, and squires were rigorously trained to serve their masters. There was a correct way to place the eating utensils and dishes, a correct way to hold a joint for the lord to carve, a correct way to eat soup (the meat and vegetables with a spoon, the broth sipped). It was considered impolite to overfill one's mouth or to belch.

Bread was baked in a communal oven not far from the castle gates; this oven was called a "four bannal," and the fact that everyone ate the bread cooked in it has resulted in the word "banal" for commonplace. The best-quality bread was called manchet, and was eaten by the lord and his family. Most bread, however, was made from rye, or from pea and bean flour. Bread also was used as a plate for meat; these thick slices of four-day-old bread were called *trenchers.* There were no such things as forks on the medieval table: knives were used only to slice off a portion, which was then eaten with the hands (for this reason it was considered essential to wash the hands thoroughly both before and after a meal, and this developed into something of a ritual). The trenchers would not go to waste after the meal, however; frequently they would be tossed to the beggars who visited many castles, on the lookout for discarded scraps.

The medieval cook was inclined to dye food curious colors. This is not so different from modern practice, although it is certain that green pork would find little favor with today's consumers. However, there were plenty of dishes that we would find most appetizing, such as venison, which was prepared in a variety of mouthwatering ways. Actually the word "venison" in the medieval period referred not just to deer but also to any hunted animal. Venison was roasted, baked, and cooked on a spit, or mixed with eggs and fruit and cooked in pies, or served with a very popular sauce called *frumenty,* made from wheat boiled with milk and eggs and flavored with saffron and sugar. On a somewhat less palatable note, the genitals and intestines also were highly prized, and were served as a dish called *haslett.*

Mealtimes were a little different from today, and also varied with the time of year. Roughly speaking, though, breakfast would be eaten as soon as one got up; dinner — the most important meal of the day — would be eaten in the late morning, after four or so hours of sunlight; supper would be at five in the afternoon, and would frequently continue well into the evening, once the beer and the wine began to flow.

During peaceful times, castles were places of rest and relaxation in which knights and liege lords could entertain important visitors, or attend to the running of their estates. However, castles also were immensely important elements in the defense of lands and kingdoms. Enemies would frequently turn their malevolent gaze on the strategic prize a castle represented, and on these occasions the banqueting and merrymaking had to cease as the inhabitants prepared themselves to endure that most terrifying of medieval war strategies: the siege.

Siege Weapons

The siege was a vitally important element in medieval warfare. Sieges were far more important than battles, and throughout the medieval period they outnumbered battles by hundreds to one. Although one might conceive of a siege as a "waiting game," with the besiegers to a castle or a town camped outside and not doing very much while they waited for the right time to attack, or for those inside to become so hungry that they threw in the towel, this is very far from the true nature of siege warfare. In fact, there was quite frenetic activity on both sides throughout a siege, as we shall see.

Although this form of warfare was practiced for many centuries, its rules and methods remained more or less constant throughout, and what changes did occur usually came from occasional advances in weapons technology and methods of fortification. The weapons of attack and defense deployed during medieval sieges were frequently ingenious and almost invariably horrifying, as were many of the acts committed during and afterward.

Siege Towers

According to the Roman architect and engineer Vitruvius, the siege tower was invented by a Thessalian named Polydus for Alexander the Great. Bradbury suggests, however, that most early forms were not towers as such, but mobile rams consisting of a wheeled platform with a roof of ox hides to protect the attackers from arrows and missiles. The medieval period saw the widespread — indeed, ubiquitous — use of proper towers, which could be very complex and elaborate affairs.

Sometimes called "belfries," siege towers had two principal purposes: the lower sections offered protection to those attempting to undermine the wall of a castle or a town, while the topmost story allowed the attackers to climb over the top of the wall. In addition, various weapons were fired from the engine, such as bows and crossbows, spears, stones, and other missiles. The siege tower also offered essential cover to mining operations — to excavate chambers beneath the wall that would weaken it, and eventually result in its collapse. This was a particularly perilous undertaking, which we shall examine in greater detail a little later.

Siege towers were constructed of wood and often were many-wheeled. They were covered with animal skins which gave some protection against missiles and burning arrows, and often were very tall. Bradbury cites the examples of an Anglo-Norman tower deployed at Lisbon that was eighty-three feet high, and another at Acre that had five stories, each of which was filled with soldiers. He continues:

> The towers at Tyre and Acre were forty, fifty and sixty cubits high; a cubit is usually said to be six feet, which would make the largest an impossible 360 feet, suggesting,

perhaps, some exaggeration here; but this may be the Egyptian cubit, which makes the highest about 103 feet, and seems possible. In any case, towers obviously could be large, since one of the main considerations was that they should overlook the walls, and at Tyre it was said: "one could look down into the city below."

Structures this massive clearly required a great deal of wood for their construction, which could be a serious problem in some regions, such as the Holy Land. There were times when the besiegers had to make do with whatever came to hand, such as in Jerusalem, where houses were dismantled and their wood used for towers; or in Tyre, where the masts and rudders of beached ships were used.

Those men capable of building such devices were obviously very highly sought after. Bradbury offers us the example of one such engineer, named Master Bertram, who was born in about 1225 and was employed as an engineer by Henry III of England. Bertram built a number of siege engines at the Tower of London and chose the oaks himself, bringing them to the tower from towns such as Reading, Windsor, and Fulham. His talents did not stop at the building of siege engines; he also designed and built some castles for Edward I in Wales.

As might be expected with tall, mobile structures, siege towers were not particularly stable, and herein lay their greatest weakness. They were especially vulnerable to heavy missiles such as rocks, not to mention incendiary weapons such as burning arrows and Greek fire. In Verdun a tower was almost toppled when the defenders attached hooks to it and rocked it to and fro. The soldiers on board fell out and were promptly attacked and killed. Also, towers could simply collapse through faulty construction, and could even be blown over by high winds.

The most dangerous phase of siege tower deployment was moving it up to the wall of the castle or town under siege, which frequently necessitated filling in the surrounding moat or ditch. At Lisbon during the Second Crusade, for instance, we see how laborious the process could be: on the first day following its construction it was moved ninety feet toward the wall near the Porto do Ferro, and a little more on the second. All the time there were archers and crossbowmen on board, and at night it was heavily defended by more than a hundred knights.

Although hugely successful as siege weapons, towers were eventually superseded by other developments in military technology. Bradbury suggests that the principal factor in this was the development of cannons, which could demolish a tower and kill all inside with a single shot.

Hurling Engines

It would not be inaccurate to describe hurling engines as the tanks of their day, their primary function being to let fly heavy missiles of various types at the walls and defenders of besieged castles and towns. One of the most powerful and impressive of these was the mangonel, a word that may derive from the Greek *mangano,* meaning "to crush." The mangonel was a mobile machine consisting of a wheeled chassis with a long arm holding a large cup. In front of the arm was a sturdy wooden bar containing a tough padded area. The beam was pulled backward until it was almost horizontal and attached to ropes that were twisted, thus containing powerful torsion energy. A rock or other missile was then placed in the cup. When the bar was released the torsion energy forced it upward until it hit the padded bar, which checked its movement; the missile would then be hurled at its target.

As with any weapon of war, positioning was of paramount importance, and hurling engines were used by defenders as well as attackers, often being placed on projecting towers to rain down destruction on the besiegers. Often, hurling engines would be placed on purpose-built mounds to increase their efficacy. As Bradbury notes, it was also very important to protect the engines against sudden attack from the defenders. He refers to James I of Aragon, who describes how during one siege, guards were required to protect hurling engines both day and night against men using grease-soaked faggots to set fire to them.

Mangonels were used most frequently during the twelfth century, and it was not uncommon for them to be deployed in large groups. According to Bradbury:

The engines used by James I of Aragon, which he called fonevols [which may derive from the Latin *funis,* meaning cord, or *funda,* meaning sling], at Lisana threw 500 stones in one night, and 1,000 in the daytime. St. Louis against Damietta had eight engines made by his Master Engineer, Jocelyn de Cornaut; and Joinville says that the Saracens had sixteen engines.

Although large stones were the most commonly used missile, there were many other types available to the mangonel crews, including lead projectiles and burning material such as Greek fire. They were also very useful in undermining an enemy's morale; it was quite common, for instance, to hurl the heads of captured soldiers over the walls. In an early attempt at germ warfare, besiegers would often hurl animal corpses and even feces over the walls to spread disease among the defenders. In fact, these tactics often spiraled out of control and resulted in horrible atrocities being committed by both sides, as when the forces of Frederick Barbarossa besieged the Italian city of Crema in 1159. During the siege, Barbarossa's men cut off the heads of their captives and played ball with them in full view of the city's defenders who, in response, dragged their own captives up to the top of the city walls and literally tore them limb from limb.

Contrary to what one might assume, the aim of these machines could be devastatingly accurate, as at the town of Saix in Spain where, during a siege by the Christians, a stone was fired from a hurling engine positioned on the roof of a tower. The stone struck a knight called Don Artal on the head, killing him instantly.

They were also powerful enough to do serious damage to the walls of castles and towns, as at Tortona in 1155, when one of Frederick Barbarossa's mangonels managed to destroy the town's upper fortifications, which collapsed upon and killed three defending knights. Smaller versions were also used aboard ships, notably by the Venetians during their attacks on Constantinople during the Fourth Crusade.

Trebuchets

Fearsome and powerful as mangonels were, they were surpassed by the counterweight trebuchet. It is difficult to say with any certainty when trebuchets were first produced; there is no documentary evidence for them before the thirteenth century. In fact, it is virtually unique among medieval siege engines in that it was invented during the period, rather than being merely a development of ancient predecessors.

Although there were later refinements, the basic design of the trebuchet was a large framework (sometimes triangular for greater stability) containing a pivoting beam, with the pivot quite far off center. At the shorter end of the beam was a large container filled with rocks, stones, lead, or other heavy materials. At the other end hung a sling into which was placed the projectile. This end was then winched down and the sling was placed flat in a shallow channel in the ground. It was held in position by a catch that, when released, would allow the weighted end to fall. The long arm then rose, and as it did so the previously horizontal sling would arc up and over the top of the arm, thus increasing the weapon's power.

As mentioned, it is extremely difficult to pin down the exact date of the trebuchet's first appearance. According to Bradbury:

Peter de Ebolus portrays a trebuchet being used in Italy at the turn of the thirteenth century, usually quoted as the first certain evidence of its existence, but in fact it is a traction trebuchet, without a counterweight. We find the appearance of a new word for these engines: *trebus, triboke, trabuchetum, trabocco,* and so on, words which become increasingly common from the 1220s. The engineer, Villard de Honnecourt, drew plans of a trebuchet in his notebook in about 1270. The elevation plan is lost, but the design shown from above survives, and shows the shape of the frame, and the positioning of the sling; 1,296 cubic feet of earth were required to fill the counterweight container, and there was a winch to lift it. The German engineer, Konrad Kyeser, at the end of the fourteenth century, also left drawings of a trebuchet, and part of his work was devoted to siege engines.

There were a number of different types of trebuchets in use by the end of the thirteenth century, although some were only very minor variations of the basic design. One, known as a *biffa,* featured a counterweight that could be moved forward and backward along the beam, thus altering the weapon's range. That range could be impressive indeed; using reconstructed trebuchets, Napoleon III demonstrated that such machines could fire a twenty-five-pound weight two hundred yards. However, the machine was useless for attacking buildings unless the right kind of projectile was used. If the stones used were too soft, they would simply shatter against a castle wall instead of damaging it. (That is not to say that they would not do considerable damage to any people they hit!)

Interestingly it was quite common for trebuchets to be given nicknames, such as Segrave, Vicar, Parson, Warwolf, and Gloucester (these machines belonged to Edward I). An Italian trebuchet at Rhodes was called the Tribute, a wry comment on the demands of the Turks to be paid a tribute. These nicknames could occasionally descend to vulgarity, as with the sling and its load of stones, which came to be known as the bollocks (which is slang in England for testicles).

Mining

Among the methods least favored by commanders, but potentially most effective in taking a castle or a town, was mining. The intention could be either simply to dig beneath the wall and emerge on the other side, or to weaken the foundations so the wall collapsed, allowing large numbers of attackers to enter at once. The latter tactic involved digging beneath a wall or a tower and supporting the gallery with timber frames, which would be set alight at the desired time. The structure aboveground would then — in theory, at least — collapse into the excavation.

Medieval commanders disliked mining because the process was unavoidably slow, and in certain instances was completely useless — for example, where a castle was built on solid rock, or was surrounded by marshland. However, when the tactic worked, it worked extremely well, and no defender could afford to ignore the potential threat of the miner or sapper, as he also was known. There were several ways of guarding against the activities of miners and foiling their efforts. Herodotus, for example, offers this episode, which occurred in 510 B.C.:

So the Persians besieged Barca for nine months in the course of which they dug several mines from their own lines to the walls, and likewise made a number of vigorous assaults. But their mines were discovered by a man who was a worker in brass, who went with a brazen shield all round the fortress, and laid it on the ground inside the city. In other places the shield when laid down was quite dumb; but where the ground was undermined, there the brass of the shield rung. Here therefore the Barcaeans countermined and slew the Persian diggers.

A variation on this method of detection was used in Europe, whereby pans of water would be placed on the ground and carefully watched; any vibration made by miners working underground would disturb the water. Of course, this method was only useful once the miners were within the walls, and if their intention was to destroy those walls, it would already be too late.

The best way to counter miners was simply to flood their mines and drown them. Alternatively, smoke could be employed, or the awful Greek fire. If all else failed, a countermine could be sunk and the defenders could go underground to fight hand to hand with the miners. Fighting in such cramped, airless, and dark environments was very unpredictable, however, and could frequently result in significant losses to the defenders.

Aboveground, the miners used a device called the cat, a mobile shelter under which they could begin their operations. Also known as sows, mice, and weasels, these structures were often attached to the base of a wall with iron nails. Mining was best performed beneath the corner of a wall, which would usually take a large chunk of wall on either side with it when it fell. This is one of the reasons why rectangular corner towers eventually gave way to circular ones, which were much more difficult to undermine.

Underground excavations could be quite elaborate, with several galleries branching off from one another, or even several levels of galleries, as in Malta. This was done to confuse the defenders and make it more difficult for them to find the attackers underground.

Scaling and Combustibles

The simplest (indeed, the most primitive) of techniques for taking a castle or a town was simply to scale the walls using ladders, some of which where constructed on the principle of the extendable lattice. Others were made of rope or hemp, with hooks at both ends. Of course, attempting to scale the walls of a well-defended fortification was extremely perilous, and countless warriors had their hands severed and their heads split in two by sword and ax as soon as they reached the battlements.

Ladders were also absurdly easy to spot, and could be pushed away from walls with ease. In addition, they could bear only a limited weight and, like poorly constructed siege towers, could collapse if too many attackers clambered up them. Once a soldier was on a ladder, he was a fairly easy target for defenders: during the siege of Smyrna in the fourteenth century one knight got halfway up a ladder, took off his helmet to see how far he had left to go, and was killed instantly by a crossbow bolt through the head.

One of the most commonly used weapons during sieges was fire. Its most straightforward application was simply burning arrows that could be shot over walls to wreak havoc within; but by far the most deadly incendiary weapon of the period was the dreaded Greek fire. This fearsome weapon was developed by the Byzantines in the seventh century. There seem to have been a number of recipes for its production, including bitumen, sulfur, resin, naphtha, and pitch. The sulfur component would make the substance stick to surfaces, while the addition of quicklime would make it ignite on contact with water. It could be sprayed from a siphon, like a modern-day flamethrower, or from hurling engines. Greek fire was used by the Turks at the sieges of Nicaea, Ma'arrat, and Acre, at which water, vinegar, mud, and even urine were used as a defense.

Bradbury offers an interesting anecdote regarding the use

of Greek fire. In 1151 Geoffrey V of Anjou was dealing with one of the leaders of a rebellion named Gerard Berlai, who possessed a castle that was said to be impregnable. Protected by a deep chasm called the Valley of the Jews, the castle had double walls and a gigantic keep. Geoffrey surrounded the castle with his own forces, enlisting the aid of the people of Saumur to drop rocks (and whatever else they could lay their hands on) into the chasm so he could get his siege towers up to the castle walls. The defenders of the castle, however, did not give up easily, and quickly repaired at night any breaches made during the day.

Geoffrey was extremely fond of books, and during this siege he read *De Re Militari* by the Roman writer Vegetius. When visited one day by a group of monks, he put the book aside out of politeness. According to the *Historia Gaufredi Ducis,* one of the monks picked up the book and began to read with interest.

> It so happened that he had come upon that section in which Vegetius Renatus explains in more detail how a tower which has been restored with joined timbers can be captured quickly. The pensive count, taking note of the old man deep and preoccupied in his reading, said: Stay with me tomorrow, dear brother, and what you find in your reading, you shall see put into practice.

Geoffrey decided to use Greek fire in his next attack on the keep the following day.

> So he ordered an iron jar, tied with iron bands and hanging from a strong chain, to be filled with the oil of nuts and the seeds of cannabis and flax. The opening of the jar was to be sealed with an appropriate iron strip and firmly locked. Then he ordered the jar to be replaced in the heated furnace for a long time until the whole thing glowed with overpowering heat, so that the

oil bubbling inside was boiling. The chain was cooled by throwing water over it, then the jar was taken out and fixed to the pole of a mangonel. With careful aim and great force, while still glowing, it was thrown by the engineers at the strong beams placed in the breaches. The contents were expelled by the impact, and the discharged matter caused a fire. Then the outflowing oil merged with the balls of fire, supplying food for the flames. The licking flames, vomiting in sudden increase, burned three houses, and hardly allowed men to escape.

Another combustible weapon was the "fire wheel." They were apparently hoops dipped in brandy and then covered with oil and gunpowder; or, alternatively, barrel hoops covered with caulking material and a very thick coating of pitch. They were then set alight and hurled at the enemy. These flaming wheels rolling toward one must have been menacing sights indeed.

Rams

Another extremely ancient but very useful weapon was the battering ram, which in its simplest form was nothing more than a large tree trunk that would be brought to bear against a wall or a gate. More elaborate versions appeared later in the Middle Ages, and these included heads that were reinforced with metal caps, and wheeled, roofed vehicles to protect the wielders from rocks, boiling materials, and so on dropped on them by the defenders. The ram itself would be suspended from ropes or chains inside its vehicle, and would simply be swung back and forth against the target.

Later rams were actually built into the lowest levels of siege towers, and were used frequently during the Crusades. As Bradbury notes, defenders deployed a number of devices against rams, some of which were rather unpleasant:

At Tyre, a Moslem officer developed an anti-ram device, catching the head of the ram with hooks using ropes from the wall, and then pulling on these to overturn the whole engine. A kind of counter-ram was developed at Tyre as well, consisting of a beam swung on pulleys using a winch, which could be aimed against the siege tower if it came close to the wall. The defenders also used pulleys to hoist up containers with dung so that they could empty it over the Franks in the tower; manning that particular tower must have been a signally unpleasant task!

Unorthodox Tactics

There were many other methods of conducting siege warfare, some of which might be considered less than fair. One of the most important was controlling the water supply, always an essential element in a siege. As we have seen, a besieging force would try to ruin the water supply of a castle or a town by contaminating it with a variety of unpleasant objects, including the rotting corpses of men and animals, and feces. Alternatively, they might try to sabotage attempts to take water from a source, such as happened at Botrum in the Holy Land, when Muslims hiding in caves within a well shaft cut the ropes of buckets lowered by Franks desperate for water.

There was also the bizarre weapon known as the crow, which defenders would lower over the castle walls and use to hook up men on the ground outside. At the siege of Malta, the Christians employed primitive handguns, some of which could shoot Greek fire. Some ideas were yet more bizarre, such as that of the sheriff of Essex under Henry III, who suggested tying combustible materials to cockerels and letting them fly over a castle's walls.

The Siege of Château Gaillard

The marriage of Henry II of England and Eleanor of Aquitaine produced four sons: two died young; the third, Richard, became known as Coeur de Lion, the Lionheart; and the fourth was John, who would conspire against his brother with his great rival Philip II of France. Born in 1157 at Oxford, Richard spent much of his youth in his mother's court at Poitiers, caring more for his family's Continental possessions than their English ones. His more or less continual absence from England was to continue when he took the English throne in 1189, spending only six months there during his ten-year reign.

Along with Philip II, Richard took part in the Third Crusade, leaving for the Holy Land in 1190. His performance was impressive, and he had an eventful trip out, conquering Messina and Cyprus and marrying Berengaria of Navarre en route to Jerusalem in 1191. He nearly took the Holy City itself from Saladin on two occasions and, together with Philip, he captured Acre. Although the Third Crusade failed in its primary objective of liberating the Holy Land from the Muslims, a truce with Saladin did result in easier access to the region for Christian pilgrims.

Philip returned to France to plot against Richard with the ambitious John. Richard owed allegiance to Philip for his Norman and Aquitaine dukedoms, and his disinclination to acknowledge this made bitter enemies of the two men. Philip therefore supported the scheming John, making a bargain with him that included John's handing over several Norman border lands.

In 1192, on his way home from the Holy Land, Richard was captured by Leopold V of Austria, with whom he had quarreled on the Crusade, and was imprisoned in the castle of Dürnstein. Leopold turned Richard over to Holy Roman emperor Henry VI, who released him in 1194, after Richard had arranged for an enormous ransom to be paid. Richard returned to England that year to crush the rebellion raised by John, before heading to France to fight Philip.

Richard built Château Gaillard (Gaillard meaning "saucy" or "cheeky") over the Seine River. In view of the castle's magnificence, it is all the more astonishing that it was constructed in only two years. It was built on a spur of ground three hundred feet high at Les Andelys, overlooking a bend in the river and utilizing the contours of the underlying rock cliffs. The design of Château Gaillard combined the traditional and the innovative: the former was displayed by its longitudinal defense, the attacker being given no alternative but to approach along a narrow peninsula, cross a moat, surmount a stout wall, take the outer bailey, cross another moat, take the middle bailey, cross yet another moat, surmount *another* wall, and then after all the casualties that would now surely have been sustained, storm a well-designed and well-defended keep.

Of the innovations of the castle, military historian Philip Warner has this to say:

> The innovations of Gaillard were not considerable enough to make it impregnable, but they were useful. Brattices, the wooden hoardings that had already proved themselves, were replaced by stone and given the new name of machicolations. Unlike later versions they were supported on buttresses, although it must have been obvious to the architects that those buttresses would prevent effective flanking fire. Below were deep battered plinths . . . which would both strengthen the structure and cause missiles to rebound and ricochet among the attackers. Every surface that could be made oblique, including the keep, was made so, in order to defeat missiles.

The outer bailey of the castle, which presented the first challenge to an attacker, was triangular in shape, its sides 175 feet in length and its base (facing the middle bailey) 125 feet long. Its walls were 11 feet thick, and each point was strengthened by a 40-foot tower. The entire castle was surrounded by a ditch 30 feet wide and 20 feet deep.

The middle bailey was approximately hexagonal in shape, once again with stout towers at its corners. It was 325 by 200 feet. The inner bailey was 100 by 200 feet and displayed another innovation: the outer wall was scalloped with 17 convex buttresses to deflect missiles. These middle and inner baileys followed the concentric method of castle design, with the inner defenses placed higher than the outer, thus allowing the defenders to concentrate fire on the approach.

Château Gaillard was constructed using conventional materials: flint rubble bound together in a cement matrix, and faced with ashlar. The already impressive natural defenses were improved upon, so that previously steep slopes were made unclimbable. It was one of the greatest architectural achievements of the time, and yet Richard did not live to see its completion; he died in April 1199 from a wound sustained during a skirmish at the castle of Chalus in the Limousin region, and was succeeded by John.

The strongest claimant to the English throne had been Arthur, Richard's nephew, but the inexperienced sixteen-year-old could not hope to counter John's subtle machinations, and he disappeared in mysterious circumstances, probably starving to death in one of John's dungeons. Philip II saw this as a perfect opportunity to move against John and, ostensibly in support of the dead boy, declared John to have forfeited his French territories.

In 1203 Philip II invaded Normandy against King John, with his sights firmly set on Château Gaillard. Apart from the castle's strategic value, John had greatly angered Philip by executing French prisoners there. Fifteen of these prisoners were blinded and sent to Philip guided by a one-eyed man. Arriving with his forces in the region, Philip immediately set about collecting reconnaissance information on the castle and surrounding landscape. His first task was, of course, to neutralize the forces defending the bridge across the first moat. According to the chronicler William le Breton, the attacking forces were rained upon with a hailstorm of stones, beams, jars of burning pitch, and lumps of iron. He continues:

> Another, as he dies, collapses in the middle of the boat on his dying comrade, and gives him his last embraces and rejoices as they go down, comrade with comrade, to the infernal regions. Another is deprived of a foot, another of his eyes, another of his ears. One falls with gushing entrails, one with his throat cut, there a thigh is shattered by a staff, here brains are scattered with a club. One man's hand is shorn off with a sword, another forfeits both knees to an axe. And still none draws back from the fight until the pitch poured from above causes them to step back. One groans as he breathes his last from a sword stroke in the face. . . .
>
> There was a huge beam at the edge of the bridgehead, a square mass of immense weight which two teams of ten bulls could hardly shift on a wagon. This, launched on them from above, surprised the two boats and shattered both prows. Then for the first time they retreated. Defeated they take to flight. In the whole army, excluding those who have not already met a violent death, there is not one whose body does not bear some wound.

One knight who was particularly brave (and a particularly good swimmer, if we are to believe William le Breton's claim that he was able to swim for miles underwater!) filled some pitchers with live coals, sealed and tarred the openings, and towed them beneath the waters of the moat until he had reached the shore and the outer ramparts of the castle. Emerging from the water, the knight started a fire that immediately gripped the wooden ligatures of the castle wall, and all those walls of the castle adjoining the town of Les Andelys, which had enjoyed the castle's protection. According to le Breton, the fire "consumed palisades, ramparts, and houses, and all scaffolding which gave protection to the walls." With their homes about to be destroyed, the townsfolk fled and took refuge in the castle.

King John made only one attempt to fight off the French besiegers. Under the command of the earl of Pembroke, the relief force was to form a double-pronged attack simultaneously from the land and the river. The timing, however, went badly wrong: Pembroke's information on the river tides was inaccurate, and the river force, which also carried food for the castle, did not arrive in time. The French were thus able to defeat each force when it arrived. John then abandoned the castle, leaving those inside to their fate.

Philip then carefully consolidated his own position, strengthening it with trenches and siege towers, blockading the castle so no new supplies could get through, and ordering his men to watch it day and night. In the meantime, he judiciously rationed his own provisions so that his army would make it through the winter with ease.

The castle was under the command of Roger de Lacy, a knight of great courage and experience, who knew immediately how serious their predicament was when he saw the French constructing their siege towers and digging their trenches. He also knew that such strenuous work would harden the bodies of the enemy yet more, so that when the assault came, it would be from men in the best physical condition.

He then committed an act that to the modern mind would seem incredibly cruel, but to a medieval commander under siege was unavoidable if he had any hope of defeating the attackers. Hitherto, the inhabitants of Les Andelys had been able to leave the castle surreptitiously at night and bring back food, but now, with the siege fully under way and the castle well and truly blockaded, their status as noncombatants made them a liability. Within a few days, de Lacy had expelled more than a thousand "useless mouths" from the castle, to take their chances among the besiegers.

The French troops allowed these poor wretches through their ranks, considering them to be utterly useless for war, and worthy more of pity than the sword. When he heard of this, however, Philip allowed no one to leave the castle, and from then on any who were expelled were immediately driven back with darts and javelins, so that they should continue to consume the castle's food, and thus hasten the day when it might fall. In fact, it was by no means a good thing to be a noncombatant during a siege: although they were sometimes allowed to leave, very often the besieging army would not allow them to pass, their own fellows would not let them back into the castle or town, and they would eventually die of slow starvation in the no-man's-land between the two forces.

This is what happened at Château Gaillard. Following the first thousand, the next batch to be thrown out by de Lacy left the castle assuming that the French would allow them to go on their way. They were horribly disappointed by the flights of spears and arrows that met them, forcing them back to the gates that, to their horror, they found closed and barred. Their sufferings were terrible, and many resorted to cannibalism as hunger began to destroy them. However, when Philip came to inspect his forward lines, the pathetic remnants of the townspeople cried out to him, begging for mercy. Philip took pity on them, for they had been reduced to such a state of weakness and despair that they could not conceivably be a threat to anyone. The French king gave them bread and allowed them to go on their way.

By February 1204 Philip decided that this costly siege had gone on long enough. Aside from the financial cost of keeping men in military service for months on end, the time was fast approaching when fields would have to be tilled and crops sown; otherwise there would be nothing for anyone to eat by the end of the year.

And so Philip began his assault on Château Gaillard by leveling the rocky ground around the outer bailey, to allow the transportation of various materials that could be used to fill in the ditches. The French also brought many hurling engines to bear, which launched all manner of missiles at the castle walls. In response to the defensive fire from arrows and spears, Philip next ordered his siege towers to be brought forward, so that his forces might fire on the defenders.

At the tops of the towers stood the finest crossbowmen the king could muster, whose bolts found many a target within the castle walls. Snipers were very active at this stage: knights on the siege towers were picked off with an arrow or a dart, and this was repaid in kind by the attackers whenever a door or a window was opened.

After much battering by trebuchet and undermining by determined sappers, the castle's outer curtain wall was breached. The wooden props in the hollowed-out chambers underground had been set alight, and the heat, combined with constant aboveground bombardment, had been more than even this massive rampart could stand. In the words of William le Breton: "It produces a great roar as it collapses . . . a cloud of smoke whirls upwards in a twisting vortex with mixed flame and smoke and the ruin belches out a great dust cloud that mushrooms out above."

In desperation, the defenders retreated from the outer bailey, the entire contents of which they set alight, so as to leave nothing that might be of any use to the attackers. The French force pursued them, but found very quickly that the middle bailey would not be nearly as easy to take as the outer had been. The ground did not permit the use of towers or hurling engines, and it seemed an impossible task to get past the moat and up the walls.

In the event massive siege engines were not needed to take the middle bailey. One of the French besiegers, a lad who showed dedication that was surely above and beyond the call of duty, managed to climb up a lavatory chute on the western side, and then in through an unfastened window in the chapel. It is somewhat ironic that the chapel, which proved to be the downfall of Château Gaillard, had not been an original part of the castle, but had been added in 1202, three years after the death of Richard the Lionheart, by his scheming brother John. Warner believes that had it not been for this feature, the castle might well have withstood the siege, although considering the apathy of King John, who abandoned it after one attempt at rescue, the inhabitants would almost certainly have been defeated by starvation sooner or later.

Once inside, the attackers made as much noise as they could, hoping to terrify the garrison into submission there and then. They were made of stronger stuff, however, and responded by setting fire to various combustibles in the hope that the smoke screen would either drive the French out, or confuse them sufficiently for them to be subdued. This was not to be, for despite the thick smoke and confusion, the storming party managed to let down the drawbridge leading to the middle bailey, and the French thundered in en masse.

The garrison had no choice but to retreat once again, this time to the inner bailey. Here, for a while at least, the castle's unusual design came into its own. The inner bailey was even harder to defeat than the middle had been; and the attackers could be sure that there were no carelessly unlocked windows in this massive wall with its convex buttresses. Even a gigantic siege engine called a Cabulus could make no impression on the walls of the inner bailey.

Once again, it was a design flaw that spelled the end for the inner bailey, although this time it was the fault of Richard and not John. Richard had left a narrow span of rock to act as a bridge over the moat, possibly (as Warner suggests) to destroy any attackers who might attempt to use it. Since it was made of rock, this bridge was all but indestructible, and thus provided cover for a team of sappers who set to work underneath it to undermine the wall of the inner bailey.

Before long, however, the mining operation was detected and a countermine was sunk within the bailey to intersect from above. The attackers were frustrated in their attempts to plant combustibles within the mine and then set it alight; nevertheless, sufficient damage had been done to the structure for the Cabulus to become effective. Eventually the weakened ramparts of the inner bailey cracked and a portion fell. Seeing this, the defenders rallied in consternation to the breach in an attempt to defend it. In their panic they neglected the sappers' tunnel, which, now unguarded, served as a very convenient avenue of entry for the French.

The garrison saw that all was now lost, and apparently for this reason they did not even bother to seek final refuge in the gigantic keep. Hunger, exhaustion, and very low morale (they had long since given up hope of rescue by the apathetic King John) had taken their toll. On March 6, 1204, the remaining 20 knights and 120 men-at-arms surrendered. King John was subsequently forced to surrender the domains of Normandy, Brittany, Anjou, Maine, and Touraine.

With Château Gaillard now in his hands, Philip began the project of rebuilding and improving the fortress. In the centuries that followed, the magnificent castle became a prison, and a notorious one at that, especially during the reign of Philip the Fair, who persecuted and destroyed the Knights Templar in the early fourteenth century. We shall examine their spectacular and bloody history in chapter 7.

Crusader Castles

With the arrival of the Crusaders in the Holy Land came the necessity of building new kinds of castles, and these magnificent fortresses have withstood the ravages of time and the harsh Middle Eastern environment for nearly a thousand years. As in Europe, these castles had more than one function: aside from being lookout posts that dominated the surrounding country, they were also supply depots and repair shops for weapons and armor. As Warner states, they were also a substitute for numbers. He goes on to supply a partial list of the first castles built by the Crusaders:

It was . . . vital to the Crusaders to build as soon as possible, and this they proceeded to do. The principles of siting remained the same as they had been elsewhere. Saphet was built in 1102 and seems to be the first of the Crusader castles. It covered the most northerly ford of the Jordan, and today is known as Safad. Toron (Tibnin) soon followed in 1116, to cover the road from Damascus to Tyre. Other castles belonging to this early period are Chastél Arnoul (El Burg), Scandelion (Iskanderun), Ile de Graye, and Saone (Sahyun), although the last of these was already in existence in a lesser form. The approach from Egypt was guarded by fortresses of Blanche Garde (Tel es Safi), Ibelin (Yibna) and Beth Gebelin.

Some of these castles fell to the Muslims, which drained the Crusaders of energy and resources. However, these castles' design became the inspiration for castles subsequently built in Europe. Perhaps the most famous of the Crusader castles is Krak des Chevaliers, which lies in the Nusaïri Mountains in southern Syria, and which was restored in the twentieth century. The castle stands on a spur cut off from the rest of a massive outcrop of rock, and separated from it by a deep trench.

The Sieges of Nicaea and Antioch

The history of the Christian presence in the Holy Land was heavily influenced by the three great sieges of the First Crusade: those of Nicaea, Antioch, and Jerusalem. We shall look more closely at the siege of Jerusalem in chapter 6; for now, let us concentrate on the others, and see how sieges were conducted in the Middle East.

The Crusaders reached Nicaea in 1097 and, despite their short supplies, began construction of siege engines for the first time. The city of Nicaea, which owed allegiance to the Seljuk sultan Kilij Arslan I, was extremely well defended, with 4 miles of walls and some 240 towers. On the western side it was defended by Ascanian Lake, which lapped against its walls, and a water-filled moat, which extended around the rest of the city's perimeter. It was essential that the Crusaders take this city, for to leave it in the possession of the Turks would endanger communications throughout the country.

The Crusaders began their campaign with a rather ineffectual blockade, which did not prevent the Turks from using the city's South Gate. The siege proper then began, with the Sicilian knights Bohemond and Tancred taking the north, Godfrey of Bouillon the east, and Count Raymond and Bishop Adhemar the south.

On May 21, Kilij Arslan arrived with his army, hoping to relieve the city. They attacked the Crusaders from the south, but they were ready and repelled the assault after a day of heavy fighting. As night fell, the sultan decided that the Crusaders were too strong, and he retreated into the mountains. The heads of those Turks who had been captured and killed were thrown into the city. This was more or less standard practice in sieges, and was intended to spread fear among the inhabitants and weaken their morale. Count Raymond then attacked the part of the city where Kilij Arslan's wife had her residence. Although he employed two siege engines, the city wall held strong, and the defenders took the precaution of piling up tons of rubble against the wall, so that even if it was breached, the attackers would find it very difficult to enter.

One of the besieged began to shout insults at the Crusaders, until Godfrey shot him dead with an arrow. Elsewhere, a particularly enthusiastic knight tried to break through a section of wall that had just been repaired. He was immediately killed and his body dragged inside the city by hooks. After removing his armor, the besieged threw his naked body back over the wall to his comrades.

The siege continued for five weeks before it was decided to attempt mining to breach the walls of Nicaea. The operation began against one of the towers, under the cover of various protective devices, including sows and a large siege tower manned by twenty knights. This latter, however, came under heavy fire from the city walls and, after much battering by heavy rocks, eventually collapsed, crushing to death all those inside.

A siege engine with a steeply sloping roof was next employed, and this fared much better. The sappers placed beams inside the tunnel they had made, and in the evening set fire to them. Unfortunately for the Crusaders, their miners chose the wrong time to fire the beams; part of the tower collapsed during the night, when the Christians were not prepared to mount an attack, and the city's defenders were able to repair the breach by morning.

Blockading the city properly was still a problem; supplies continued to get in via the lake. The Crusaders sent word to Byzantine emperor Alexius I requesting that he send boats so they might intercept these supplies. For the lake he provided a flotilla, which the Crusader knights dragged overland from the sea. According to the chronicler William of Tyre, some of the boats were dismantled, each being placed on three or four wagons drawn by oxen, and then hauled the seven miles to the lake during the night, to be reassembled on the shores the next morning.

The sight of these ships on the lake finally persuaded the people of the city to negotiate terms of surrender, after a siege lasting just over seven weeks. This was fully in accordance with Alexius's wishes, for he knew that a ruined city was no good to him; and in any event, most of the inhabitants were Christians, the Turks comprising only the soldiers and a small group of nobles.

The capture of Nicaea was of great importance to the

Crusaders, providing a considerable return on the initial expenses of mounting the expedition to the Holy Land. Of yet greater value, however, was the city of Antioch, which would provide an excellent strategic base for their operations. In addition, this former Roman city had only recently been captured by the Muslims, in 1085.

The city of Antioch was founded in 300 B.C. by Seleucus I of Syria, and named after his father. Lying on the Orontes River twelve miles from the sea, it was immensely important, being the principal city in Asia and, under the Roman Empire, the third city in the world. It was one of the holiest places on Earth to the Christians: not only was it the place where they had first been called by that name, but also St. Peter had founded his first bishopric there. According to the chronicler William of Tyre, the city was defended by four hundred towers and two miles of walls. It was surrounded by marshy land to the north, with the river to the east and mountains to the south. Within the city walls stood two peaks, the higher of which stood a thousand feet high, and at the summit of which was a citadel.

Antioch was ruled by Yaghi-Siyan, who had been informed of the presence of the Crusaders and had stored a large amount of supplies in anticipation of the siege he knew must surely come, since they would not be able to march south to Palestine unless the city was firmly in their hands. The Crusaders arrived in the vicinity of Antioch in 1097, and discussed the pros and cons of beginning the siege at once. It was winter, and the cost of waiting until the spring could be high, since the town was sure to receive more supplies during that time and thus would be even harder to conquer. Thus the Crusaders decided to begin the blockade immediately; they had plenty of supplies from Nicaea, in addition to which they had just taken the Iron Bridge across the Orontes and captured a convoy of cattle, sheep, and grain intended for Yaghi-Siyan's army. The Crusaders were very well provisioned, for the moment.

As they looked upon the city the Crusaders could not fail to be impressed with its magnificence. Sir Steven Runciman, in his wonderful *History of the Crusades,* offers a vivid picture of Antioch:

The houses and bazaars of Antioch covered a plain nearly three miles long and a mile deep between the Orontes and Mount Silpius; and the villas and palaces of the wealthy dotted the hillside. Round it all rose the huge fortifications constructed by Justinian and repaired only a century ago by the Byzantines with the latest devices of their technical skill. To the north the walls rose out of the low marshy ground along the river, but to the east and west they climbed steeply up the slopes of the mountain, and to the south they ran along the summit of the ridge, carried audaciously across the chasm through which the torrent called Onopnicles broke its way into the plain, and over a narrow postern called the Iron Gate, and culminated in the superb citadel a thousand feet above the town. Four hundred towers rose from them, spaced so as to bring every yard of them within bowshot. At the north-east corner the Gate of St. Paul admitted the road from the Iron Bridge and Aleppo. At the north-west corner the Gate of St. George admitted the road from Lattakieh and the Lebanese coast. The roads to Alexandretta and the Port of St. Symeon, the modern Suadiye, left the city through a great gate on the river-bank and across a fortified bridge. Smaller gates, the gate of the Duke and the Gate of the Dog, led to the river further to the east. Inside the *enceinte* water was abundant; there were market gardens and rough pasture ground for flocks. A whole army could be housed there and provisioned against a long siege. Nor was it possible entirely to surround the city; for no troops could be stationed on the wild precipitous terrain to the south.

The Crusaders set about preparing for their blockade of the city, cutting down the orchards to clear an approach and using the wood to construct siege weapons. Several knights stationed their men at strategically important points: Bohemond, prince of Taranto, took the Gate of St. Paul; Raymond IV of Saint-Gilles the Gate of the Dog; and Godfrey of Bouillon the Gate of the Duke. The remaining armies took up stations behind Bohemond to await instructions. They also built a bridge of boats across the Orontes, which gave them easy access to the roads to Alexandretta and St. Symeon. Work was also begun on two siege towers: one, called Malregard, facing the Gate of St. Paul; the other, commanded by Tancred, facing the Gate of St. George.

Raymond suggested that they should storm the city immediately, but the other commanders decided it would be better to wait for reinforcements, which included (so rumor had it) a fleet of Genoese ships. Bohemond, however, had other reasons for wishing to wait before attacking Antioch: he intended to possess the city himself, and preferred not to see it stripped of its riches by his comrades. His intention was to find intermediaries through whom to forge connections with the city's inhabitants, and thus to arrange for it to surrender to him alone.

Bohemond's plan was aided by the situation within the city. The inhabitants were mostly Christians, Greeks, Armenians, and Syrians. Yaghi-Siyan had been tolerant toward the Christians, allowing the Orthodox patriarch, John the Oxite, to remain there and even forgoing the conversion of the churches into mosques. However, when it became clear that Antioch was next on the list of the Crusaders' targets, Yaghi-Siyan responded by imprisoning John the Oxite and expelling the leading Christians from the city. Many others fled after witnessing the desecration of the Cathedral of St. Peter, which was turned into a stable.

Due to the gaps in the city's defenses, these exiles kept in contact with their relatives who were still inside, and had few qualms about sharing information with their fellow Christians who were besieging the city. However, as Runciman reminds us, "many of the local Christians, in particular the Syrians, doubted whether Byzantine or Frankish rule was preferable to Turkish." They therefore decided to keep Yaghi-Siyan just as well informed about the Crusaders as they were about him.

Further emboldened by the Crusaders' reluctance to attack immediately, Yaghi-Siyan ordered his men to creep out from the western gate and attack any small group of Crusaders they found. By this time, the condition of the besiegers had deteriorated: their hitherto plentiful supplies had dwindled to almost nothing, and illness was taking its toll. The Crusaders were able to repel a Turkish relief attempt, after which they conducted a little exercise in psychological warfare, hurling two hundred Turkish heads over the city wall from siege engines. It was then that Godfrey of Bouillon performed a feat that was to become legendary. Having already decapitated many an enemy with a single stroke, Godfrey swung his sword at another adversary and cut him cleanly in half. The part of his body above the waist fell to the ground, while the lower part remained on his horse and was carried into the city.

In mid-November the rumors regarding the Genoese fleet proved to be true. Thirteen ships arrived at the port of St. Symeon, bringing men and arms. The food problem remained, however, and many men deserted the camp, including Peter the Hermit, on whom history has passed a far harsher judgment than his fellows ever did (see chapter 6). Peter was accompanied by a carpenter named William, who had already deserted a military campaign in Spain. The two of them were pursued by Tancred, who dragged them back to the camp in shame. Peter enjoyed a high reputation among the Crusaders, and so was discreetly pardoned; William, on the other hand, was made to stand all night in Bohemond's tent before receiving a threatening dressing down.

It was through the treachery of a single man that the city

of Antioch finally fell to the Crusaders. On the western side of the city wall stood the Tower of the Two Sisters, which was controlled by a captain named Firouz, and which was faced by Tancred's siege tower. According to the chronicler Anna Comnena, daughter of the Byzantine emperor Alexius I, Firouz was an Armenian who had converted to Islam, and with whom Bohemond had established contact during the siege. The reason for Firouz's betrayal was his anger with his master, who had fined him for hoarding grain.

Although Firouz was suspected of being a traitor by his fellows, who knew of his antagonism toward his master, he managed to persuade them otherwise by suggesting that the city's defenses be strengthened yet more. For his part, Bohemond kept his contact with Firouz to himself, letting no one in on the secret, and emphasizing the terrible dangers in attempting to take the city. He added a request that, should he himself manage to achieve the virtually impossible and get the Crusaders into Antioch, he be allowed to keep the city for himself.

At this point, news reached the Crusaders that the Turkish general Kerbogha of Mosul was fast approaching with a vast relief army, prompting another wave of desertions, including a knight named Stephen of Blois, who thought it pointless to wait around to be slaughtered. On the day of Stephen's departure, Firouz sent his son to Bohemond to say that all was ready. It is believed by some (based on the account given by William of Tyre) that Firouz was vacillating between loyalty and treachery, until his wife was discovered by their son in the arms of one of the Turkish rulers of the city.

The plan was for the Crusaders to head eastward, as if to intercept Kerbogha's approaching army, only to double back under cover of night and return to the western wall, where Firouz would be waiting for them in the Tower of the Two Sisters. Bohemond called a meeting with Adhemar de Monteil (the Bishop of Le Puy), Raymond, Godfrey, and Robert of Flanders, who all agreed to the scheme.

The Crusaders made a great show of leaving the city for the east, lulling the inhabitants into a false sense of security. By the early hours of the following morning, they had returned and arrived at Firouz's tower. A ladder was placed against the tower, and sixty knights climbed up in silence and entered the room where Firouz was waiting for them. They quickly took the other two towers under Firouz's control, which allowed the knights on the ground to scale the sections of wall between. While some knights proceeded along the walls to take other towers, their comrades headed into the city itself and threw open the Gate of St. George and the Gate of the Bridge, on the other side of which the main Crusader force was waiting.

Once inside the city the Crusaders joined forces with the Christian, Greek, and Armenian inhabitants, and together they massacred every Turk they could find, including women and children. Awakened by the screams of the dying, Yaghi-Siyan went to find his bodyguard and fled the city through the Iron Gate. However, his son Shams ad-Daula was made of stronger stuff, and instead of running for his life made his way with a few loyal men to the citadel perched high above the city.

Seeing this, Bohemond gathered his own forces and attempted to take the citadel, but without success. He was wounded, and his men decided it was far more worthwhile to loot the city than waste time with the citadel. Yaghi-Siyan, meanwhile, had been thrown from his horse in the mountains outside the city. His escort continued their flight, leaving him behind to be discovered by some local Armenian Christians, who immediately killed him and sent his severed head back to Antioch, where Bohemond received it with satisfaction.

By the end of the day Antioch contained no living Turk. The invaders continued to move from house to house, taking what they wanted and destroying what they did not. So many had been massacred that one could not walk through the streets without treading on their lifeless bodies.

This was not quite the end of the story, for Kerbogha's army had arrived outside Antioch, and Shams ad-Daula and his men still held the citadel. The Crusaders thus found themselves facing their enemies in two directions. They began by building defenses between themselves and the citadel, and barely managed to repel an assault by the Turks outside, who had by that time completely encircled the city. Once again, food became scarce, and the knights and pilgrims were forced to eat leaves, thistles, dried horse skin, and even carrion and seeds of grain found in manure.

Amid all this hunger, disease, and misery, some knights envied Stephen of Blois for having had the good sense to leave when he did. In fact, many chroniclers condemned him for what they saw as inexcusable cowardice, although this seems unlikely since, as Bradbury notes, the leaders of the Crusade had elected him commander in chief of their forces shortly before his departure. Bradbury writes:

> Reading between the lines it seems most likely that Count Stephen's mission was to go to the emperor [Alexius] and seek aid for the crusaders at Antioch. If he described the situation as desperate, that was hardly an exaggeration. The count seems to have left before Kerbogha closed in, and once that had occurred, it would have been nearly impossible for anyone outside to know the true position. It seems very likely that the emperor's refusal to continue his march on Antioch [it was already known that he had started out from Constantinople] had less to do with Stephen's pessimism, than with the information that Kerbogha and a very large army was now outside the town. The emperor's decision to turn back left Stephen in an impossible situation; without the emperor and his army the count was in no position to relieve Antioch, or even to get back in. His decision to return to the West was not an heroic one, but is not difficult to understand.

According to the chroniclers who vilified him (including Orderic Vitalis and Anna Comnena, who clearly wished to protect her father's reputation), Stephen returned to the West and his wife, who was the daughter of William the Conqueror, and who was so horrified by his lack of mettle that she insisted he go back to the Holy Land immediately. Bradbury has serious doubts about the veracity of this story, and notes that Stephen lost no time raising new forces and returning to Outremer, to die bravely fighting the Turks.

In June 1098, a peasant named Peter Bartholomew, servant of a Provençal pilgrim, presented himself at Raymond's tent. Peter claimed to have received visions over several months from St. Andrew in which he was told of the location of the Holy Lance that had pierced the side of Christ during the Crucifixion. Peter told Raymond and the bishop of Le Puy that he had been praying one night when an old man with silver hair appeared to him, claiming to be St. Andrew. Peter was then "taken" to the Cathedral of St. Peter inside the city, to the southern chapel, where the old man descended into the ground and reappeared carrying the Lance. He then told Peter to return to this spot with twelve companions when the city had been taken.

Bishop Adhemar de Monteil was less than impressed by this bizarre tale. After all, the Holy Lance resided at Constantinople, its claim to authenticity long established; how could it lie here as well? Raymond, however, was far more enthusiastic, and stated that a search would be made for the Lance at the location mentioned by Peter. On June 14 the Crusaders watched as a meteor fell to Earth, apparently right on top of the Turkish camp. The following morning, Peter was taken to the location he claimed for the Lance, accompanied by twelve others, including Raymond, the bishop of Orange, and the chronicler Raymond of Aguilers.

Workmen toiled all day, digging a deep pit but finding nothing of any interest. Undaunted, Peter leaped into the pit and held up a piece of iron. News of this miraculous discovery quickly spread among the Crusaders, although Adhemar still considered Peter to be a charlatan, and to have buried the object himself at an earlier date, possibly during the cleaning and reconsecration of the cathedral.

Others shared the bishop's doubts, which so infuriated Peter that he demanded to be allowed to undergo an ordeal by fire, walking through flames while holding the relic. The ordeal took place on April 8, 1099, Good Friday. It seems that the Lance did not protect him as he hoped it might, for he was horrifically burned and died in agony a few days later. Nevertheless, the relic was still believed by many to be genuine, and its effect on their morale was not lost on their leaders, who declared a five-day fast as penance for their sins. The knights were already on the verge of starvation and, as Bradbury wryly notes, "it is not surprising that the Christians had hallucinations, and saw St. George and an army of saints on white horses coming to their aid."

The final battle for Antioch took place on June 28. The Crusaders, divided into thirteen battle squadrons, assembled at the Gate of the Bridge. Bishop Adhemar's squadron carried the Holy Lance as a talisman. The Turks who were still holding the citadel watched these preparations in trepidation and signaled to Kerbogha, who dispatched his horse archers to harass the Crusaders while he deployed his main force. The tactic failed; the archers were routed by the Crusader infantry, who then returned to face the main force of the Turks.

Kerbogha sent a detachment of cavalry to a nearby hiding place, with the intention of bringing them up behind the Christians to force them to fight on two fronts. This force now charged Bohemond and his men, who nevertheless managed to hold firm until Godfrey and Tancred came to their aid. The Turks were no match for the Crusader knights, some of whom were mounted, some of whom were on foot, and all of whom thrust and slashed at their enemies in a chaos of blood and steel. Seeing that his army was in the process of being annihilated, Kerbogha ordered some of his men to set fire to the dry grass upwind of the Crusaders. This desperate strategy worked to a certain extent: amid the thick smoke, some Crusaders who were on foot were pounced on and killed; but it had little effect on the mounted knights, who simply galloped away from the blinding cloud and continued their rout of the Turks.

At this point, Kerbogha accepted that the day was lost, and with it Antioch. He retreated to the east, accompanied by his surviving forces. The city was finally in the hands of the Christians, and the way to Jerusalem was open.

6

The Fall of Jerusalem

The Birth and Early Life of Godfrey

Godfrey of Bouillon, the Crusader knight who would become the ruler of Jerusalem amid an ocean of blood, was the second son of Eustace II, duke of Boulogne, and Ida of Bouillon, daughter of the duke of Lower Lotharingia. There is a story — probably apocryphal — that when a woman of the ducal household saw that the child was hungry and began to breast-feed him, his mother snatched him from her and made him vomit. Enraged at the presumptuousness of the woman, Ida told her that any milk but her own would dilute the child's nobility. Whether true or not, the story provides some insight into the mind-set of the nobility at the time, a nobility that was engaged in a complex melee of fragile and mutually suspicious alliances that ruled territories in England and France.

Eustace II was a Norman warlord famed for his enormous mustache, and who was fond of decorating his helmet with strips of whalebone. According to the explorer and historian Tim Severin: "It is not clear whether he chose this crest because whales were popularly considered to be terrifying monsters who swallowed ships entire, or because whale fishery was a primary occupation of the [English] Channel port from which he took his title." A well-judged first marriage to a woman twice his age made him brother-in-law to Edward the Confessor, king of England, and a cousin by marriage to the Duke of Normandy, and this secured Eustace not only a number of lands and fiefs in England but also the opportunity to fight on the side of William the Conqueror at the Battle of Hastings.

His son Godfrey had been born about six years earlier; there is very little information on his early life, or indeed even where he was born. Since his father held a large amount of land in France and his mother had estates in Belgium, it could have been in either of those countries. As Severin reminds us, in those days infant mortality was horribly high, and very few details of a child's life were recorded until it was reasonably certain that the child would survive to adulthood. He continues with another tale that, like the breast-feeding anecdote, may or may not be true:

> [Godfrey] and his two brothers, Eustace the older and Baldwin the younger, had scampered into the duke's chambers and were hiding beneath the skirts of their mother. Their father asked flippantly what was making the commotion. "Three princes," his wife is reputed to have replied, "the first will be a duke, the second a king, and the third a count."

Like her husband, Ida was descended from Charlemagne, and was the daughter of Godfrey the Bearded, a fascinating and colorful character who is worthy of a book in his own right. He constantly plotted against the German emperor, who was his feudal overlord, who imprisoned him, took away all his estates, and ultimately forced him to flee for his life to Italy, where, undaunted, he married Beatrice, who just happened to hold the richest duchy in the country. Ida herself was renowned for her piety and generosity to the church, and it is most likely that she instilled in the young Godfrey the sense of religious devotion that was to carry him to the Holy Land, and the ultimate prize of Jerusalem, the Holy City itself.

When Charlemagne died in 814, his empire, known as the Kingdom of the Franks, covered much of Europe. A few decades later, the territory had been divided among his descendants, the eastern part becoming the Kingdom of Germany and the western part the Kingdom of France. The third section was ultimately absorbed by Germany and France, its northerly segment becoming the dukedoms of Upper and Lower Lotharingia, both of which were in the possession of the German king and could be presented to the vassal of his choice, in accordance with the rules of feudalism at the time.

Ida's father, Godfrey the Bearded, had laid claim to both these dukedoms (one of the many acts that had made him so disliked by the German emperor). By the time he died in 1069 he had secured Lower Lotharingia for his own family. As we saw in chapter 1, the training of a noble for knighthood began at an early age, and Godfrey was no exception. In his case, the road to greatness began when it was decided that he should serve his apprenticeship with his uncle Godfrey the Hunchback, duke of Lower Lorraine, who was without male heirs.

He received his training for knighthood at Château Bouillon, of which Severin offers an evocative description:

> Day-to-day life, by our modern standards, was a quirky mixture of discomfort and occasional luxury. Château Bouillon had not yet been expanded into its later size and was merely a sturdy round tower of massive stones, with several floors and a conical wooden roof that made the building look like a squat pencil stub set on end. Privacy was virtually unknown. All life took place at ground level in the circular main hall, its floor covered with rushes, bare of furniture except for a few trestles and

tables. Here lived, ate and slept all the duke's immediate retainers — men-at-arms, clerks, servants, grooms, and hangers-on as well as the cluster of squires and pages. Heat and smoke came from a fire in the centre of the room which must have made life on the upper floors very sooty. Light, what there was of it, leaked in through small windows that were mere holes-in-the-wall in summer, and blocked with oiled paper or cloth in winter. Access to the upper floors, where the Duke had his personal chambers, was by a wooden stair at the side of the hall, but only privileged members of the household would ascend unless the castle was under attack: then the main defence was conducted from the top of the tower and its galleries.

When Godfrey the Hunchback was assassinated in 1076 the dukedom of Lower Lotharingia did not pass directly to Godfrey the Bearded, but rather to the son of his liege lord, the Holy Roman emperor Henry IV. Godfrey was left — for the moment, at least — with only the marquessate of Antwerp. For the next eleven years, however, as a vassal of the German emperor, Godfrey sided with the army of Henry IV in the War of the Investitures, and followed the emperor on his expedition to Italy against Gregory VII (1080–1084). In the interval he was forced to return to defend his possessions against the count of Namur, and in about 1089 Henry IV restored to him the legacy of Godfrey the Hunchback by creating him duke of Lower Lorraine, following the elevation of Henry's young son to the title of king of the Romans.

According to the chronicler William of Tyre, Godfrey was a religious man, mild-mannered and virtuous. He was just, trustworthy, and dependable in his undertakings. "He scorned the vanities of the world, a quality rare in that age and especially among men of the military profession. . . . His whole life was commendable and pleasing to God." He was taller than average, extremely strong, with stout limbs and a handsome face. His hair and beard were medium blond, and he was considered to be outstanding in the use of weapons and in military strategy.

Taking the Cross

Godfrey's decision to leave behind the comfort of his vast dukedom and head for battle and the likelihood of a violent death in the strange lands of Outremer was influenced by two important factors. The first was the plea to the Christian West for help, which came from the emperor of Byzantium, Alexius Comnenus. At the time, the Seljuk Turks were spreading rapidly outward from their homeland in central Asia, and were overrunning the Byzantine provinces of Anatolia. Alexius was only too aware of the terrible threat posed by the Seljuks, since Byzantium had already met them in battle under the leadership of his predecessor, Romanus Diogenes. The imperial army had been surrounded by Seljuk cavalry in the Manzikert Valley in Anatolia and annihilated.

The Byzantine Empire was desperately short of soldiers, and was having to rely on mercenaries in its dealings with the Seljuks. Alexius decided to appeal to the piety of Christian Europe, and sent representatives to the first great council of Pope Urban II, held in March 1095 at Piacenza. The pope and his bishops were impressed by the appeal of the Byzantine ambassadors, not least because they felt that a march to defend the Holy Land from the infidels would unite the quarrelsome knights of Europe in a higher cause.

At the Council of Clermont in November 1095 Urban told the assembly of the woes experienced by their Christian brethren in the East, how they were routinely beaten and robbed and their shrines desecrated by the infidels. He paid special attention to the sufferings of the thousands of pilgrims who journeyed to Jerusalem every year. Following this, Urban made his appeal for Western Christendom to aid its brothers. He promised that, should they stop fighting and killing each other and turn their attention instead to the great work of making righteous war against the Turks, God would forgive them all their previous sins. He contrasted the strife and spiritual poverty of life in the West with the glory of true friendship with God that would be their reward in the Holy Land.

Urban was an eloquent and powerful orator, and the response to his words was immediate and unequivocal. Even while he was speaking, cries of *"Deus le volt!"* (God wills it!) rose from the gathering. As soon as the pope had finished, Adhemar de Monteil, the bishop of Le Puy, stood up, approached the papal throne, and, falling to his knees, begged to be allowed to join the expedition. The Pope blessed him and the many other volunteers who came forward, pledging their lives in the service of God.

Later, Urban drew together his bishops again, and it was decided that the worldly belongings of all those who should join the Holy War must be protected by the church until they returned. Every knight should also wear a red cross on his surcoat as a sign of his dedication to the great cause. The expedition still needed a leader, and Urban nominated Adhemar, who had been the first to pledge himself.

The first noble knight to join was Count Raymond of Toulouse, who sent a message to Clermont informing the pope of his and his knights' eagerness to take the Cross. (At that time, the expedition was not referred to as "the Crusade," but simply as "taking the Cross" or "taking the Way of God.") As he was the first nobleman to take the vow, he believed it was his right to be given the secular leadership of the other knights. Urban was not amenable to this, and so Raymond decided to cooperate with the wise and tactful Adhemar.

Urban then traveled throughout Western Europe, preaching the Crusade and exhorting all who heard him to take the Cross. Possibly at Raymond's suggestion, he also sent letters to the powerful maritime republic of Genoa, asking for its cooperation. The republic provided twelve galleys and a transport, which set sail in July 1097. The pope's travels yielded spectacular results, with news coming from all over Europe, including Scotland, Denmark, and Spain, of knights who had pledged themselves to the Cross.

The second factor that influenced Godfrey's decision to take the Cross was much closer to home. His administration of Lorraine had not been very efficient, and Henry IV began to wonder whether he had made the right decision in granting it to him. Godfrey was well aware of this, so it was partly from doubts about his future in Lorraine and partly from genuine enthusiasm that he answered the call to the Crusade. He and his brothers were joined by many leading knights from Walloon and Lotharingian lands: their cousin, Baldwin of Rethel, lord of Le Bourg; Baldwin II, count of Hainault; Rainald, count of Toul; Warner of Gray; Dudo of Konz-Saarburg; Baldwin of Stavelot; Peter of Stenay; and the brothers Henry and Geoffrey of Esch.

The whole of northern France had been roused to action by the letter of Pope Urban II beseeching the French nobility to join the Crusade to the Holy Land. Together with his two brothers, Eustace and Baldwin, Godfrey was among the first knights to take the Cross in 1096, and to forsake the land of his birth for the searing heat and time-drenched landscapes of the cradle of his faith. To secure the resources necessary for his journey, Godfrey sold or pledged many of his estates, and was greatly pleased that so many nobles immediately arrayed themselves beneath his banner. In August 1096 he departed at the head of ten thousand knights and thirty thousand foot soldiers, composed of Walloons and Flemings. Born at the frontier of the two nations and speaking both languages, he served as the link between them, while his authority served to appease the quarrels provoked by their national self-esteem.

Thus was the great wheel of the First Crusade set in motion by Alexius Comnenus's plea for help from his Christian brothers. However, his intention had been to enlist aid in the protection of his eastern frontier, not to march all the way to Jerusalem to wrest it from the hands of the Muslims who had controlled it for the previous 450 years. To Western Christendom, the situation demanded vigorous action: their Holy City was under threat from the infidel, and with it their very faith. The fate of Byzantium was seen very much as secondary to the fate of Jerusalem.

The Massacre of the Jews

The army led by Godfrey was one of four that set out for the Holy Land; of the other three, two had been raised in France and one in southern Italy. The plan was for them to leave in the spring of 1096, the individual knights joining their overlords and then journeying on to meet their commanders (of whom Godfrey was one). As each army continued on it would gather more volunteers until all four reached Constantinople at year's end. Then, so they thought, Alexius would join them with his own forces and together they would march to Jerusalem.

The nobility was not the only section of medieval European society for whom the call to take the Cross was too powerful to ignore. The peasantry also responded in their thousands, selling their meager possessions to raise money for the journey. According to one historian of the Crusade, an abbot named Guibert, who had been present at the Council of Clermont: "[T]he poor were soon inflamed with so burning a zeal that none stopped to consider the slenderness of his means, neither whether it was wise for him to leave his house, his vines and his fields; and each set about selling the best things he had for a price much less than if he had found himself cast into the most cruel captivity." He goes on to describe the pitiful sight of the poor desperately trying to prepare adequately for their chosen course: "Truly astonishing things were to be seen, things which could not but provoke laughter; poor people shoeing their oxen as though they were horses, harnessing them to two wheeled wagons on which they piled their scanty provisions and their small children, and which they led along behind them."

This pitiful rabble was a far cry from Pope Urban's vision of a disciplined expedition composed of trained knights, but, as Severin comments, once the call to take the Cross had been heard, the situation quickly spiraled beyond his control: "The crusading message was taken up by all manner of fanatics, and self-appointed heralds began to spread their own version of his call among the lay people."

One such fanatic was an unsavory little character known as Peter the Hermit, on account of the hermit's cape he habitually wore. According to Sir Steven Runciman, the preeminent authority on the Crusades:

> He was a man of short stature, swarthy and with a long, lean face, horribly like the donkey that he always rode and which was revered almost as much as himself. He went barefoot; and his clothes were filthy. He ate neither bread nor meat, but fish, and he drank wine. Despite his lowly appearance he had the power to move men. There was an air of strange authority about him.

Peter's preaching found many converts among the poor of northern Europe, whose lives had been blighted by disease and famine and who were very open to the apocalyptic teachings he espoused. As Runciman reminds us, medieval people were convinced that the Second Coming was close at hand, and that their sins could be expiated through pilgrimage. Moreover, in their ignorance the peasants confused Jerusalem with the New Jerusalem, and believed that to enter the city would be to enter the Kingdom of God itself.

The peasants' fervor was increased even more by a series of natural phenomena that they mistook for signs that God was watching their efforts with approval. In the spring of 1095 there was a shower of meteorites, and the following year the moon turned red during an eclipse. Added to this were numerous rumors of crosses appearing on men's skins. These events combined to whip the bucolic rabble into a religious frenzy. At this point they began to question the need to travel all the way to Jerusalem to do God's work and destroy the sinner. There were plenty of God's enemies in Europe, their ringleaders declared: it was the Jews who had been responsible for Christ's death; surely they were worse than the Muslims, and much closer to home.

Word of this dangerous attitude quickly reached the Jewish communities of northern France, and they were sufficiently alarmed to write to their fellows in Germany, warning that the Crusaders were likely to cause serious trouble for them. Peter the Hermit took speedy advantage of this fear, obtaining letters of introduction from the French Jews to Jewish communities throughout Europe, asking them to welcome him and his followers and supply them with provisions. In return, he assured them that they would receive no trouble from his "Crusaders."

Tragically, their safety was very far from assured. In April 1096, a man named Volkmar took ten thousand men from the Rhineland to join Peter the Hermit. A few days later another army, led by an old disciple of Peter's, Gottschalk, entered Bavaria. A third army also was on the move, led by Count Emich of Leisingen, who claimed to have been mysteriously branded with a cross. With eyes more firmly set on personal profit than religious devotion, Emich ordered his followers to attack the Jewish community at Spier. Following this, Emich and his brigands arrived at the town of Worms, and a rumor soon began to circulate that some Jews had drowned a Christian and were using water tainted by his decomposing corpse to poison the town's wells.

The people of the town and the surrounding countryside decided to take their revenge and attacked the Jewish quarter. The bishop of Worms intervened on the Jews' behalf, offering his palace as a sanctuary to them. Ignoring his pleas, Emich and the townsfolk broke into the palace and slaughtered all five hundred people inside. This massacre was repeated at Mainz less than a week later. From there, Emich proceeded to Cologne, which had seen anti-Jewish riots the previous month. Here, however, the Jews were hidden and protected by their Christian friends. Two Jews were killed and the synagogue burned to the ground, but further bloodshed was avoided.

Emich then decided to make for Hungary, but a large number of his followers broke away and headed for the Moselle Valley, with the intention of killing the Jews there, most of whom were given refuge by the archbishop in his palace. The force then moved on to Metz, where they killed twenty-two Jews. When they returned to Cologne with the intention of rejoining Emich, they found him gone. Some then returned home, their "Crusade" completed, while others joined Godfrey's army.

Volkmar and his army arrived at Prague in late May and within a few days began to massacre the Jews in that city. He then marched into Hungary and attempted more atrocities against the Jews there, but the Hungarians counterattacked and scattered Volkmar's mob. Gottschalk and his men entered Hungary at Wiesselburg, and immediately began to pillage the countryside, stealing all manner of animals and produce. The Hungarian peasants resisted, and a Hungarian boy was impaled alive. The Hungarian king Coloman surrounded the Crusaders with his troops at a village called Stuhlweissenburg, disarming them and taking back all they had stolen. It is unclear whether they tried to resist, or whether news reached King Coloman of the atrocities they had already perpetrated; whatever the reason, the Hungarian army massacred the Crusaders and their leaders.

A few weeks later Emich arrived at the Hungarian frontier with his men and asked Coloman's permission to pass through his territory, a request that the king understandably refused. Emich would not take no for an answer, however, and fought with the Hungarians for six weeks, with his men eventually forcing their way to the fortress of Wiesselburg and laying siege to it. The garrison made a sortie into the Crusaders' camp and defeated them utterly. Emich and a few knights were able to escape, and returned to their homes.

Coloman

The route to the Holy Land Godfrey decided to take was that followed by the other Crusader leaders, through Hungary. For Godfrey, this had the added attraction of being the route taken by his great ancestor Charlemagne on his pilgrimage to Jerusalem. He left Lorraine in August 1096, and at the beginning of October arrived at the Hungarian frontier on the Leitha River. Godfrey then sent a small group of knights, headed by his ambassador Geoffrey of Esch, to King Coloman to ask for permission to cross his territory.

King Coloman was a remarkable man who was known throughout Europe for his literary knowledge and great intelligence. So great was his learning, particularly in the field of theology, that he was known as Coloman the Bibliophile. In addition, he was a warrior of considerable prowess, which he proved in no uncertain terms in his routing of the murderous rabble who had caused so much suffering and bloodshed in France and Germany. Some of the survivors, on encountering Godfrey and his men, had brazenly lied about their experiences, claiming they had been savagely mistreated by the Hungarian king.

Coloman, of course, was far from enthusiastic about playing host to more Crusaders. Nevertheless, he received Godfrey's envoys with courtesy, taking the opportunity to explain to them exactly why he had acted so harshly against the "pilgrims" who had entered his country. After keeping Godfrey's envoys for eight days, he announced that he would grant Godfrey himself an interview at his court. He sent a letter to Godfrey: "From the King Coloman to the Duke Godfrey and all the Christians, greetings and most sincere regards. We have heard that you are a man of power and a prince on earth, and those who know you have always appreciated your trustworthiness. This is why, knowing your unusual reputation, I now wish to meet you and make your acquaintance."

At their meeting near the inland sea called the Neusiedl, the two men discussed the outrages perpetrated by the peasants, and Coloman was impressed by Godfrey's behavior and bearing. Godfrey stayed with Coloman for one week, while they negotiated the Crusaders' transit through Hungary. The duke of Bouillon gave his word that his men would behave themselves and give no trouble to the people of Hungary, in return for which Coloman promised to supply them with the provisions they would need at an inexpensive price. Notwithstanding the trust that was growing between the two men, Coloman considered it prudent to ask Godfrey to agree to two safeguards: first, that the Crusaders would allow themselves to be escorted through the country by the Hungarian army; and second, that a hostage of Coloman's choice should be delivered to him, to remain until the Crusaders had left the country.

Coloman decided that Baldwin (whom the king rightly considered to be potentially dangerous) should be left with him as a hostage, together with his wife and children. After an initial refusal (to which Godfrey replied that he would therefore be obliged to offer himself as a hostage instead), Baldwin rather shamefacedly agreed to give himself and his family over to Coloman's court. After provisioning, the Crusaders passed through Hungary without incident (Godfrey having warned them that any misbehavior would be punished by death), and Baldwin and his family were released without harm once the army had crossed the Sava to Belgrade.

Once again, the army passed peacefully through the Balkan peninsula, and at Philippopolis received news that Hugh of Vermandois had arrived at Constantinople. Hugh, the brother of the king of France, had been shipwrecked on the Adriatic coast and sent to Constantinople. The rumors regarding Hugh's reception in the city were somewhat at odds with each other: some stated that he and his men had received marvelous gifts, while others reported that he was a prisoner. According to Severin:

> If Count Hugh was not exactly a prisoner, nor was he entirely free to leave the city. He was, as matters would turn out, the first of a number of pawns which the astute Alexius would put on the board as he matched wits with the succession of Crusader armies advancing on his terrain.

Godfrey Arrives at Constantinople

In early December Godfrey's army arrived at Selymbria on the Sea of Marmara. Here its hitherto exemplary discipline broke down completely, and for eight days the army ran riot across the countryside. This sudden savagery was Godfrey's response to the evasive reply he had received from Alexius when he sent a message demanding Hugh's release.

On December 23 Godfrey's army arrived at Constantinople and, at the request of Alexius, camped outside the city. Having been informed of the pillaging in the countryside beyond the city, Alexius was most anxious that Godfrey give him his oath of allegiance and move on as quickly as possible, so he sent Hugh of Vermandois to see him. Hugh seemed quite happy and unharmed, and yet Godfrey was extremely reluctant to give his oath to Alexius: after all, he had already sworn an oath of loyalty to Henry IV, and in addition he was anxious to consult with the other Crusader leaders, who had yet to arrive in the city.

Hugh thus returned to the emperor without an answer from Godfrey. Alexius was angry, and made the mistake of attempting to punish Godfrey by cutting off the supplies he had already promised to supply for the army. Baldwin responded instantly by raiding the suburbs of Constantinople. These hostilities might have escalated were it not for the time of year: it was realized on both sides that Christians should not be fighting each other at Christmas, and so Godfrey reigned in his men and agreed to move his camp to the Golden Horn, the sea inlet that lay to the north of Constantinople. Here they would be sheltered from the winter winds, and the imperial police would be able to watch them more closely. As a token of his own goodwill, Alexius allowed traders to visit the camp and sell provisions.

The emperor then repeated his invitation for Godfrey to visit him, but the knight still mistrusted him, and was still eager to consult with the other Crusader leaders who were on their way. However, not wishing to provoke Alexius further, he sent his cousin, Baldwin of Le Bourg; Conon of Montaigu; and Geoffrey of Esch to the palace in his stead. He again hesitated to give his oath of allegiance, and in March of the following year Alexius's patience finally ran out. Not only did he forbid the traders to sell provisions to the Crusaders, but also, in their stead, he sent Turcopoles (Turkish mercenaries) across the Golden Horn. The Crusaders, of course, were unaware of this, and when they saw the boats arriving at the shore, they assumed more food had arrived. Instead, they were greeted by arrows, and several of them were killed.

Godfrey was outraged at this development and immediately decided to attack Constantinople. In the company of five hundred of their finest knights, Baldwin moved to the only bridge over the upper end of the Golden Horn, aiming to secure it. The Turcopoles were ready for them, however, and once again let fly their arrows. The battle that followed lasted all day, with the Turcopoles aided on several occasions by imperial troops who sortied from the city.

It did not take the knights long to realize the strategy the imperial forces were following: Alexius had ordered his troops to target the knights' horses rather than the knights themselves. The reason for this was straightforward enough. In the words of his daughter Anna Comnena:

[W]hen fighting and warfare are imminent, inspired by passion [the Franks] are irresistible (and this is evident not only in the rank and file, but in their leaders too), charging into the midst of the enemy's line with over-whelming abandon — provided that the opposition every-where gives ground; but if their foes chance to lay ambushes with soldier-like skill and if they meet them in a systematic manner, all their boldness vanishes. Gener-ally speaking, [they] are indomitable in the opening cav-alry charge, but afterwards, because of the weight of their armour and their own passionate nature and reck-lessness, it is actually very easy to beat them.

In addition:

[E]very Frank is invincible both in attack and appear-ance when he is on horseback, but when he comes off his horse, partly due to the size of his shield, and partly to the long curved peaks of his shoes and a consequent difficulty in walking, then he becomes very easy to deal with and a different man altogether, for all his mental energy evaporates as it were.

And so the Byzantine archers concentrated their fire on the horses, maiming and killing them, and leaving the knights without their most valuable piece of equipment, and unable to pursue the archers as they retreated into the city following each attack. Nevertheless, the imperial forces failed in their efforts to scatter the Crusaders; and the Crusaders, lacking siege engines, were in no position to mount a serious assault on Constantinople. This stalemate lasted for the next six days, with the Crusaders looting the outlying suburbs.

On April 3 Alexius again sent Hugh of Vermandois to ask Godfrey to take the oath of allegiance to him, suggesting that his troops cross over to Asia even before he had taken the oath. Godfrey again lost his temper and threw his forces at the city. This time, however, the Byzantine response was too powerful for the Crusaders, who fled from the onslaught. Godfrey himself finally realized that he had no real choice but to take the oath and allow his army to be transported across the Bosphorus.

The last thing Alexius wanted was for the entire Crusade (of which Godfrey's vast army was only a part) to meet outside the walls of Constantinople; his intention was to transport each group of arrivals across the Bosphorus and get them as far away from his city as possible. Godfrey and his entourage were taken into the city by boat, dressed in their finest regalia in a rather naive attempt to impress the Byzantines. They were unprepared for the sheer splendor of Constantinople. Later, the chronicler Fulcher of Chartres would write of his own astonishment in breathless prose:

> Oh what a great and beautiful city is Constantinople! How many churches and palaces it contains, fashioned with wonderful skill! How many wonderful things may be seen even in the streets or courts! It would be too tedious to enumerate what wealth there is of every kind, of gold, of silver, of every kind of robes, and of holy relics.

Godfrey and his men were taken through the magnificent city to the Blachernae Palace, close to the outer wall. The fantastic beauty of Constantinople was echoed in the emperor's residence, which contained marble-paved courtyards and gold and jewels wherever they looked. The fabulous riches that were so ostentatiously displayed were intended to impress the visitor with the emperor's wealth and power, for, as Severin notes, "did he not have all the resources to pay great armies, bribe his enemies, hire allies, or reward his friends?"

Of course, the Crusaders' finery could not hope to compare with that of the emperor, who received them in jewel-encrusted robes of incredible sumptuousness. Nor were the Crusaders' manners much to be proud of: Anna Comnena describes with the utmost distaste how, at one point, one of the lords walked up to the imperial throne and sat himself down on it. The emperor was too polite to say anything, and it was left to Baldwin to angrily order the offending knight, whose name was Latinus, to stand up immediately, saying: "You ought never to have done such a thing, especially after promising to be the emperor's liege man. Roman emperors don't let their subjects sit with them. That's the custom here and sworn liege men of His Majesty should observe the customs of the country."

In her description of the episode Anna continues:

The man said nothing to Baldwin, but with a bitter glance at Alexius muttered some words to himself in his own language: "What a peasant! He sits alone while generals like these [the visiting Crusaders] stand beside him!" Alexius saw his lips moving and calling one of the interpreters who understood the language asked what he had said. Being told the words he made no comment to the man at the time, but kept the remark to himself. However, when they were all taking their leave of him, he sent for the arrogant, impudent fellow and asked who he was, where he came from and what his lineage was.

The knight replied that he was "a pure Frank," and that he was undefeated in single combat; indeed, there were very few who even dared meet him in such circumstances. Alexius replied gracefully with some tactical advice on how to avoid being massacred by the Turks.

The emperor made good his intention to buy Godfrey and his men and get them away from his realm as quickly as possible. According to Albert of Aix, the emperor made the following flattering but highly ambiguous proclamation to Godfrey:

> I have heard that you are a most mighty knight and prince in your land, a man most prudent and of perfect trust. In the presence of this multitude and more to come, I therefore take you for my adopted son; and all that I possess I place in your power that through you my empire and lands may be saved.

According to Severin:

This of course was nonsense. Either the Franks did not understand exactly what the Emperor was saying or, more likely, he was choosing his phrases to mislead them. Designing ambiguous statements that could be interpreted in any number of ways was a high art-form in the Byzantine court, and the announcement was a meaningless formula which allowed Alexius to claim that [Godfrey] was now his vassal. Godfrey kissed the Emperor's hand, as did the other nobles, and the presents, or rather bribes, were immediately brought out and distributed. There was gold and silver for all, purple cloth, mules and horses. Every week thereafter, while Godfrey's army was close to the capital, four men went from the palace treasury to the Duke's camp carrying a sum in gold besants sufficient to pay his troops' expenses. This money, declared Albert [of Aix] wonderingly, the Duke distributed entirely, keeping nothing for himself. In effect the Lotharingians were on the imperial pay roll.

In February 1097, Godfrey made good on his word to take his forces over the Bosphorus. With one group of Crusaders finally out of the way, Alexius awaited the next, led by Bohemond, whom Anna Comnena detested with all her heart, believing him to be deeply dangerous and dishonest. "In everything," she wrote, "in his words as well as his deeds, he never chose the right path." She believed that Bohemond intended to seize her father's empire; but on this occasion he arrived at Constantinople with only ten men. Anna believed he had left the rest of his forces behind so that he could ingratiate himself with the emperor. In the event Bohemond was persuaded by Godfrey to offer his own allegiance to Alexius.

The Battle of Dorylaeum

It has been claimed that the single most decisive event of the First Crusade was the Battle of Dorylaeum, which saw the opposing forces of Christianity and Islam meet head on. Following the taking of Nicaea, the Crusaders made their way across Asia Minor on the Byzantine main road, which extended south from Chalcedon and Nicomedia, and joined the road from Helenopolis and Nicaea. From the Sangarius River it climbed through a valley and over a pass to the city of Dorylaeum. Here the road split into three. The first went east, crossing the Halys River and branching toward Armenia, Caesarea Mazacha, the Anti-Taurus Mountains, the Euphrates Valley, and the Cilician Gates. The second road extended from Dorylaeum across the salt desert at the center of Asia Minor, an incredibly hostile environment entirely lacking in water and only passable by travelers who could move very quickly. The third road extended along the southern edge of the salt desert, from Philomelium to Iconium and Heraclea.

Dorylaeum was the unavoidable starting point for the Crusaders' journey across the country, and on June 26, 1097, the Crusaders began to march toward the city in the company of a small Byzantine force under the command of the Byzantine general Taticius. Those warriors who had been wounded at the siege of Nicaea stayed behind and, under the command of General Butumites, set to work repairing the stronghold. At the village of Leuce, the leaders of the Crusader force decided to split the army into two divisions, which would travel one day apart, thus easing the problem of supplies. According to Runciman:

> The first army consisted of the Normans of southern Italy and of northern France, with the troops of the Counts of Flanders and of Blois and the Byzantines, who were providing the guides. The second army included the southern French and the Lorrainers, with the troops of the Count of Vermandois. Bohemond was regarded as the leader of the first group and Raymond of Toulouse of the second. As soon as the division was made, Bohemond's army set out along the road to Dorylaeum.

In the meantime, Sultan Kilij Arslan, who had lost Nicaea (and with it a sizable portion of his wealth), forged an alliance in the east with the Danishmend emir. In late June the sultan made his way westward with new forces, including Cappadocian Turks and the Danishmend army. They reached a valley close to Dorylaeum and prepared for battle.

On the evening of June 30 the first Crusader army set up camp outside Dorylaeum, and at dawn the Muslims attacked. According to the anonymous knight who wrote *Gesta Francorum* (The Deeds of the Franks) and who was present at the battle: "Our men could not understand whence could have come such a multitude of Turks, Arabs, Saracens and other peoples whose names I do not know, for nearly all the mountains and hills and valleys were covered with this accursed folk."

However, the surprise implicit in this statement does not seem to have been shared by Bohemond, who acted with impressive speed to gather the noncombatant pilgrims in the center of the Crusader camp, both for their own safety and to act as water bearers from the springs there to the warriors on the front line. At the same time, a messenger was sent back to the second army to tell them of the threat and to join the first as quickly as possible.

Bohemond instructed his captains to remain on the defensive initially and not to risk men in direct assaults. One knight, however, disobeyed these orders: Latinus, the same upstart who had committed such a terrible faux pas at Constantinople. Anna Comnena seizes the opportunity to pour scorn on him in her *Alexiad:*

> That crazy idiot, Latinus, who had dared to seat himself on the imperial throne, forgetting the emperor's advice stupidly rode out in front of the rest (he was on the extreme end of Bohemond's line). Forty of his men were killed then and he himself was seriously wounded. He turned in flight and hurried back to the centre — visible proof, although he would not admit it in words, of Alexius' wise counsel.

The Crusader camp was soon completely surrounded by Turkish forces, and the commanders began to wonder whether they would be able to withstand the constant rain of arrows that fell upon them from the lightning-fast Muslim archers. Part of the camp was overrun by Turks, who killed every pilgrim they could find, the noncombatants being no match for those fearsome mounted warriors. Fulcher of Chartres wrote of those horrific moments: "All of us huddled together like sheep in a fold, trembling and terrified, were fenced in by the enemy on all sides, so that we could not turn in any direction." Many pilgrims ran to their priests to make what they were certain would be their final confessions.

For his part, Bohemond continued to apply the only sensible tactic in view of his position: to try to hold off the Turkish assaults until the second Crusader army appeared. As discussed in chapter 3, the favored tactic of the European knight was the *chevauchée,* or mounted assault. However, this could not work against the Muslim archers on their swifter horses. The initial assault might well prove successful in scattering the enemy and leaving their supply trains vulnerable to capture; but once they had come to a halt, their horses now tired and their attention fixed on whatever booty they could acquire, they themselves would be open to attack from the enemy archers. Bohemond was experienced enough to be well aware of this, and ordered his men to maintain their defensive positions.

The author of *Gesta Francorum* shared his fellows' admiration of the battle prowess of the Turks and wrote: "What man, however experienced and learned, could write of the skill and courage of the Turks. They have a saying that they are of common stock with the Franks, and that no men, except the Franks and themselves are naturally born to be knights." He continued: "The Turks came upon us from all sides, skirmishing, throwing darts and javelins and shooting arrows from an astonishing range."

The Christian crossbowmen replied as best they could but, as we noted in chapter 3, these weapons took time to reload and prime. Anna Comnena came to the same conclusion:

He who stretches this warlike and very far-shooting weapon must lie almost on his back and apply both feet strongly against the semicircle of the bow and with his two hands pull the string with all his might in the contrary direction. In the middle of the string is a socket, a cylindrical kind of cup fitted to the string itself . . . and through this arrows of many sorts are shot out. The arrows used with this bow are very short in length, but very thick, fitted in front with a very heavy iron tip. And in discharging them the string shoots them out with enormous violence and force, and whatever these darts chance to hit, they do not fall back, but pierce through a shield, then cut through a heavy iron corselet and wing their way through and out the other side.

As Severin notes, the time taken to reload meant that for every shot a crossbowman managed to get off, a Turkish archer could fire several arrows *and* take himself out of range.

The battle was not going at all well for the Crusaders, almost all of whom received wounds of varying seriousness, and watched helplessly as the Turkish arrows found them, their comrades, their horses, and the noncombatant pilgrims. So disheartened were some of the foot soldiers that in the afternoon many of them retired to the civilian camp to hide in the tents. Luckily for them and the civilians, the Turks who were rampaging through the camp assumed that they had come to engage them, and immediately retreated.

In the meantime, the messenger sent by Bohemond to find the second army came upon them and told them the grim news that the first army was under attack from the Turks and, unless help arrived very soon, would be destroyed. Godfrey acted without hesitation, ordering the war horns to be sounded as he, Count Raymond of Toulouse, and Bishop Adhemar took to their horses and left their camp. The foot soldiers, of course, could not hope to keep up with the mounted warriors, and were told to get to the battlefield as quickly as possible. Albert of Aix offers us a vivid picture of Godfrey and the others heading at full speed to aid their comrades:

Already a very clear day had dawned, the sun was shining with brightest rays, and its splendour flashed on the golden shields, and the iron mail. The standards and flags, shimmering with jewels and purple, raised on high and fixed on spears, were fluttering. The swift horses were urged on with spurs, nobody was waiting for companion or friend but each going as fast as he could, they pressed on their way to the assistance and revenge of the Christians.

By the time the relieving force arrived at midday, those under attack had come to accept the likelihood that they would have to face martyrdom: retreat was impossible, and the only other alternative, capture and slavery, was unthinkable. When it seemed that all was lost, the commanders of the second army were sighted, Godfrey and his knights first, and then Raymond and his.

This was something of a shock to the Turks, who believed that they had surrounded the entire Crusader force; the last thing they expected was a whole new army to descend on them. Taken by surprise, the Turks hesitated at the crucial moment, and were unable to prevent the two Christian armies from reaching each other and consolidating their forces. The Crusaders were as relieved as their enemies were dismayed and immediately established a long front facing the Turks, and bolstered their renewed enthusiasm still further by speculating on the amount of treasure they would secure in the event of a victory.

Runciman suggests that at this point the Turks were not only demoralized but also were probably running short of ammunition. In any case, they despaired yet further when they saw Bishop Adhemar and a contingent of southern French soldiers appear on the hills behind their positions. This rear action, combined with the forward push of the main Crusader force, resulted in the breaking of the Turkish lines. Godfrey launched his own attack, while the reinforced Christian line prepared itself for the *chevauchée*, which could now succeed, given the number of Crusaders present and the chaos into which the enemy had been thrown.

Writing of this maneuver, Severin declares:

The momentum of thousands of knights cantering or galloping as a great inchoate mass was unstoppable.

Together each horse and rider might weight in excess of a ton, and the chivalry, travelling forward shoulder-to-shoulder, amounted to a cataract of muscle and bone, iron and steel. There was nothing refined or sophisticated about the manoeuvre. The horses knocked down opposing footmen or barged into the enemy mounts. Each knight thrust first his lance and when that was torn from his grasp or he had come to close quarters, he swung his heavy sword. Unless his opponent was similarly mounted, the contest was very one-sided. The sweep of the great sword depended on a stable platform, and the larger and steadier the horse the more formidable became his rider. . . . In strategic terms Dorylaeum was the military climax of the First Crusade. That day, as never again, there were more knights assembled, more battle horses, more cohesion and more vigour than at any other time on the great journey.

Utterly routed, the Muslims fled to the east, leaving behind all their tents and the possessions they contained. Although great, the victory had been hard won, and paid for with the lives of many Christians. Runciman states that the Franks had been taught to pay proper respect to their Turkish enemies, although he adds that this willingly given admiration of the fighting prowess of the Turks did much to enhance the Crusaders' own victory.

From his position in the civilian camp, which included the Crusaders' supply train, Fulcher of Chartres had a less than perfect view of the later events of the battle. In fact, he displays some confusion as to the reason for the Turks' sudden flight. Nevertheless, he describes how the Crusaders gave chase to their fleeing enemies, eventually coming to their tents and the treasure contained within.

The way across Asia Minor was now open to the Crusaders. Sultan Kilij Arslan had lost not only his capital city but also his royal tent and with it most of his treasure and

supplies. The Crusaders found themselves in welcome possession of gold and silver, as well as numerous horses and
sheep. They also discovered several camels, which they had
never seen before. During his flight east Kilij Arslan encoun-
tered a group of Syrian Turks on their belated way to the
now-concluded battle. He informed them that all was lost,
that the Frankish numbers had been simply too great. They
then decided to ruin the surrounding towns and countryside
so the Crusaders would find it difficult if not impossible to
feed themselves on their continuing journey east. According
to the unknown author of the *Gesta Francorum,* the Turks
"burned or destroyed everything that might be useful or
helpful to us as they fled in great terror at our approach."

The Crusaders rested for two days at Dorylaeum, recover-
ing from the battle, planning the next phase of their journey,
and basking in the glory of their victory. A rumor spread that
two angelic horsemen on radiant mounts had been seen just
before the battle commenced, and this confirmed to the
Crusaders that their endeavor had the blessing of God Himself. At this point they decided not to split up the army again,
a tactic that had brought them so close to disaster the last
time; instead, they would march as a single unit. They had
three alternative routes on which to continue their march to
the Holy Land. The first was the military road to the east,
but this extended well into territories that were still controlled by the enemy, including the Danishmends. The second route was the road that ran directly across the great salt
desert; however, this also was out of the question, since the
Crusader army could not hope to be able to move quickly
enough, and would certainly perish of thirst long before it
reached the other side. The only possible choice was the road
that skirted the desert on its southern edge; but even this
presented its own perils. It was a war-torn region whose villages had been destroyed, whose fields had not been culti-
vated for years and that were therefore useless, and whose
wells had long ago run dry or their waters become tainted.

What was left of the population could be counted on to flee in terror from anyone they laid eyes upon, and so would be a less than useful source of information.

On July 3 the army moved out from Dorylaeum, heading southeastward toward Polybotus and then turning toward Pisidian Antioch, where it hoped to secure fresh supplies. They then rejoined the main road at Philomelium, and entered the war-scarred, desolate landscape that lay between the mountains and the great salt desert.

Of this strange and horrible place, the *Gesta* knight had this to say: "We pursued [the Turks] through a land which was deserted, waterless and uninhabitable, from which we barely escaped alive, for we suffered greatly from hunger and thirst and found nothing at all to eat except prickly plants which we gathered and rubbed between our hands." The only water was the undrinkable brine of the salt marshes, and the contents of the old Byzantine roadside wells that had been tainted by the retreating Turks.

William of Tyre comments on the European animals that the knights had brought with them out of habit and that could not hope to survive in this formidable climate.

Delicate birds, soaring hawks and falcons, with which the nobility is wont to take delight when hunting and hawking, breathed forth their lives notwithstanding the care lavished upon them. . . . Keen-scented dogs trained for hunting, the pets of their lords, deserted their masters whom they had ever faithfully followed and panting from thirst, succumbed along the route.

Sad as the loss of these beloved animals was, of much greater seriousness was the toll taken on the Crusaders' horses. Many knights were forced to proceed on foot, or on oxen; and sheep and goats were used as beasts of burden to pull the baggage trains. Many people likewise perished from exhaustion and thirst, although the most heartrending and pitiful sight must surely have been the sufferings endured by pregnant women, whose bodies were ravaged by the unendurable heat of the sun, and some of whom gave birth and had no choice but to abandon their offspring on the road.

Albert of Aix describes how the pilgrims tried pathetically to take moisture from the early-morning mists that they drew desperately into their lungs. He adds that to come upon a source of drinkable water could, ironically, be just as lethal as to be deprived of it. When they reached a river, he writes, many threw themselves headlong into the waters and drank uncontrollably, filling their parched and withered stomachs until their bodies, unable to cope with the sudden shock, expired at the very moment of their salvation.

By the middle of August the Crusaders had reached Iconium, in the middle regions of the country. In the beautiful valley of Meram the Christians rested for some days, gathering the strength that had all but deserted them. Here Godfrey sustained a serious injury. He and some of the other nobles found a wood, and decided to do a little hunting. Armed with swords, bows, and arrows, they entered the wood. According to Albert of Aix, Godfrey went off on his own, and before long came upon a pilgrim who had been gathering twigs and was now running for his life from an enormous bear. Godfrey instantly drew his sword and spurred his horse toward the animal, which lashed out at him, driving its claws through his tunic and hurling him to the ground. The fearsome beast

> embraced him in his forepaws as he fell from his horse, and hastened to tear his throat with his teeth. The Duke therefore in great distress, remembering his many distinguished exploits and that he had up till now markedly escaped from all danger, indeed lamenting that he was to be choked by this bloodthirsty beast in an ignoble death, and seizing the sword which had got entangled in his own legs in the sudden fall from his horse and the

struggle with the frenzied wild beast, and holding it by the hilt aimed swiftly at the beast's throat, but mutilated the calf and sinews of his own leg with a serious cut.

All this while, the peasant had been screaming for help and, drawn by his cries, a man named Huscechinus came upon them. Drawing his own sword, he fell upon the bear, and he and Godfrey (with blood pouring from his wounded leg) managed to kill the frenzied animal. In hideous agony Godfrey was taken back to the Crusader camp, where he was treated by their doctors amid the "grief of the men, and howling of the women."

When Godfrey had recovered and the other Crusaders had rested sufficiently, the army headed for the valley of Heraclea, where they found a Turkish force, under Emir Hasan, waiting for them. The Crusaders, led by Bohemond, immediately attacked and scattered the enemy, who fled to the north.

Once again, it became necessary to discuss the route ahead. The most direct way led across the Taurus Mountains, through the Cilician Gates, to Antioch. However, this route had many dangers, not least of which were the narrowness and steepness of the road through the Cilician Gates, which would make the slow-moving Crusaders and pilgrims vulnerable to attack. In addition, it was September, and the climate, according to the Byzantine guides, was truly awful. The memory of their recent journey was still fresh in the Christians' minds, and they had no desire to experience such miseries again.

A far more attractive alternative was the road to Caesarea Mazacha, which led across Anti-Taurus to Marash and the plain of Antioch. Another advantage of this route was that it passed through territories held by Armenian Christians, who would certainly be friendly. And so, in the second week of September, the main army set off toward Caesarea and, at the village of Augustopolis, intercepted Emir Hasan's forces, which it once again defeated.

After reaching Caesarea the Crusaders continued to the town of Comana, which the Danishmend Turks were besieging. At the arrival of the Crusaders the Danishmends fled, and the citizens welcomed their fellow Christians with open arms.

The Crusaders then moved southeast to Coxon, which also was inhabited by Armenians. Again, the Crusaders were welcomed, and were able to fully reprovision themselves. They remained there for three days, resting and preparing themselves for the arduous trip across the Anti-Taurus Mountains. At this time a rumor reached them that the Turks had abandoned Antioch. Raymond of Toulouse realized that if this were true, he would have to act quickly, so he sent five hundred knights ahead to occupy the city.

These knights, led by Peter of Castillon, headed for Antioch. However, when they stopped at a castle held by Paulician heretics near the Orontes River, they learned that the rumor was false and that, far from abandoning Antioch, the Turks were sending additional soldiers to make it even more impregnable.

The Crusaders' journey from Coxon over the Anti-Taurus Mountains began in October, and was everything they had feared. The season of rain had begun, and the road across the mountains, already in a dreadful state, was made even more treacherous by the incessant downpour. For much of the journey, they had to negotiate narrow tracks with bare rock on one side and steep cliffs on the other. The animals fared worst: many horses lost their footing and tumbled over the edge, as did the pack animals, which were roped together. The heavy equipment carried by the knights became first a hindrance and then a curse, and many threw their weapons away.

Eventually the horrific trek ended, and the Crusaders found themselves in a valley that contained the Armenian city of Marash. Once again they took the opportunity afforded by a friendly reception to rest and recuperate. On October 15 the army left Marash and headed toward Antioch.

The Siege of Jerusalem

At that time, Jerusalem was one of the world's greatest fortresses. Its walls had been added to and improved through the centuries by Hadrian, the Byzantines, the Ommayads, and the Fatimids. The eastern wall was protected by the ravine of the Kedron, while on the southeast the ground fell away sharply to the Vale of Gehenna. The western wall was skirted by another valley that was only slightly less deep. The only points that favored an attack were on the southwest wall, which cut across Mount Sion, and along the length of the northern wall. Although there were no springs within the city, there was an ample water supply in the enormous cisterns.

Responsibility for the city's defense lay with the Fatimid governor, Iftikhar ad-Dawla, who took the sensible precaution of blocking or poisoning the wells outside the walls when he heard of the Crusaders' approach. He also sent an urgent message to Egypt for armed aid.

Upon their arrival the Crusaders immediately took up positions in areas where the land at least allowed them to approach the city walls. Robert of Normandy took the northern wall opposite the Gate of Flowers (Herod's Gate), while Robert of Flanders took his station at the Gate of the Column (the Damascus Gate). Godfrey of Bouillon took the northwestern angle of the city, where he was joined by Tancred, who arrived with flocks he had taken from Bethlehem.

The siege of Jerusalem began on June 7, 1099. The advantage lay with the besieged, who were well supplied with food and water, and who were able to strengthen the city's towers with sacks of cotton and hay, thus enabling them to withstand the assaults of the Crusaders' mangonels. The Crusaders soon had great difficulty with their water supply: Iftikhar's poisoning of the wells turned out to be a most effective tactic. The only available source of pure water came from the pool of Siloam below the southern walls, which was dangerously exposed. The only alternative was for the Crusaders to send out soldiers and pilgrims into the surrounding landscape to find water, which left them open to attack by small companies from the city. In addition, the besiegers began to run out of food, while their armor caused them even more discomfort in the fierce heat of the Judean summer.

On June 12 some of the Crusaders made a pilgrimage to the Mount of Olives, where an old hermit told them that if their faith were strong enough, they should attack the city the next day. This they did, but although they succeeded in breaching the defenses of the northern wall, they had too few ladders to scale the walls simultaneously in a sufficient number of places. After several hours of fighting they finally withdrew.

The Crusaders decided to postpone further attacks until they had built siege machines capable of penetrating Jerusalem's defenses. The only problem was that they had no material with which to construct them. On June 17, however, six Christian vessels (two Genoese galleys under the command of the brothers Embriaco, and four English ships) put into the harbor of Jaffa. Hearing that the ships had arrived, and were carrying the food and materials they so desperately needed, the Crusaders sent a small detachment to the harbor. The troops were ambushed near Ramleh by a Muslim company from Ascalon, and were saved only by the arrival of Raymond Pilet and his men, who had been following them.

At this point reinforcements arrived from Egypt in the form of a fleet that blockaded Jaffa. However, the cargo had already been unloaded from the Christian vessels, and they were abandoned, their crews marching with Raymond Pilet to the camp outside Jerusalem. Although the ships had brought food, armaments, ropes, nails, and bolts, they had not brought any wood with which to construct the necessary siege machines, so expeditions were sent out for miles around to search for what was needed. Eventually Tancred and Robert of Flanders entered the forests around Samaria and returned with logs carried by camels and captured Muslims. Immediately the Crusaders started building scaling ladders, while Raymond and Godfrey began work on a wooden castle fitted with catapults and wheels.

Early in July the Crusaders learned that a large army had set out from Egypt to relieve Jerusalem. They knew that they had to take the city quickly, but their morale was extremely low due to the suffocating heat and the lack of adequate food and water. On the morning of July 6, the priest Peter Desiderius went to his lord, Isoard of Gap, with a strange story. He had seen a vision of Bishop Adhemar, who had fallen ill and died while the Crusaders were at Antioch. The bishop had ordered them all to fast and to walk in procession barefoot around the walls of Jerusalem. If they did this with repentant hearts, they would take Jerusalem within nine days. Bishop Adhemar's instructions were obeyed; a fast was undertaken that lasted for three days, following which a procession moved slowly around the city. The bishops and priests led, carrying crosses and holy relics, followed by the princes and the knights, and finally the foot soldiers and the pilgrims. All were barefoot, and were mocked by the Muslims who gathered atop the city walls.

The Crusaders drew great strength from this, and in spite of their thirst worked hard and with enthusiasm to complete the great siege towers. On July 10, the wooden structures were complete and were wheeled into position against Jerusalem's mighty walls.

Rivers of Blood

It was decided that the attack should begin on the night of July 13–14. It would be launched simultaneously from Mount Sion and on the eastern sector of the northern wall, with a feint attack on the northwestern angle. The fighting strength of the Crusader army was twelve thousand foot soldiers and twelve hundred to thirteen hundred knights. First the assailants filled in the ditch around the city walls, while the defenders poured Greek fire and hurled stones on them, and their own mangonels answered with heavy bombardment.

By evening Raymond's men had wheeled their tower over the ditch and against the wall. But Iftikhar himself commanded this sector, and Raymond could not establish a foothold on the wall. The following morning, Godfrey's tower stood against the northern wall, close to the Gate of Flowers, with Godfrey and his brother Eustace commanding from the upper story. By midday they had made a bridge from the tower to the top of the wall, and the best fighters of the Lotharingian army were led across by two Flemish knights, Litold and Gilbert of Tournai.

Once one sector of wall had been captured, it was much easier for the assailants to use their scaling ladders to climb into the city. Godfrey stood on the wall, directing the invaders and sending men to open the Gate of the Column to the main force, while Tancred and his men penetrated deep into the streets. Seeing that their defenses were broken, the Muslims retreated to the temple area (the Haram es-Sherif), which contained the Dome of the Rock and the al-Aqsa Mosque. Their intention was to use the al-Aqsa Mosque as a last fortress, but they had no time before Tancred was upon them.

Realizing that all was now lost, they surrendered to Tancred and promised a huge ransom for their safety; they even took his banner to display over the mosque, as a sign that they were now under his protection. Elsewhere in the city, Iftikhar was still holding out against Raymond; but by the early afternoon he, too, realized that the Crusaders could no longer be held at bay, so he withdrew into the Tower of David, which he promised to hand over, along with a huge amount of treasure, in return for the lives of himself and his bodyguard. Raymond accepted, took possession of the tower, and ordered that Iftikhar and his men be allowed to leave the city unmolested.

The Crusaders ran riot throughout the city, sparing no one, not even those who thought that Tancred's banner would protect them. Men, women, and children were slaughtered. The massacre lasted all day and throughout the night, and it is said that by the morning the streets were filled with dismembered corpses, and the victors waded through rivers of blood that were knee-deep. The Jews also were slaughtered, since they were held to have aided the Muslims. It is uncertain just how many people died in the fall of Jerusalem, but there is no doubt that the city was all but emptied of its Muslim and Jewish inhabitants.

Avocatus Sancti Sepulchri

The massacre at Jerusalem was utterly horrific, and disgusted many even among the Crusaders. The streets were filled with decaying corpses, which soon became a health hazard, so the Arabs who had survived and been taken prisoner were forced to drag the putrefying bodies of their fellows to the city walls and throw them over. The Crusaders had swept through the streets like a torrent of death, entering houses, butchering their occupants, and announcing their ownership of the property by hanging a shield or a flag outside the door.

Exactly what role Godfrey played in these atrocities is not entirely clear: William of Tyre states that he was at the forefront of the murderous mob, while Albert of Aix claims that he was unable to control the blood lust of his men. According to Albert, so horrified was Godfrey at what he saw before him that he took off his armor, replaced it with a simple woolen garment, walked barefoot to the Church of the Holy Sepulchre, and gave thanks to God for placing the Holy City in their hands.

Indeed, as might be expected, the Crusaders believed

wholeheartedly that God had been on their side, and that it was due to His intervention that the Crusade had succeeded, and Jerusalem was now a Christian city. They even claimed to have seen a divine figure standing on the Mount of Olives beckoning to them during the attack. When the city finally fell, others swore that they had seen the ghostly figure of the dead Bishop Adhemar walking through the streets, in the company of many of their comrades who had succumbed to the rigors of the long journey from Europe.

In his book *Crusader,* Severin notes:

> The accusation that the First Crusade was largely motivated by territorial greed is contradicted by the fact that no one, not even among the barons, seemed to have any ready-made plan for Jerusalem once it was captured. There was no notion whether Churchmen or barons should be responsible for the Holy City, or who would be the overall leader. Not until a week after the fall of the city did the council assemble to choose who should hold Jerusalem.

Intent on providing a new king for the conquest, the Crusaders offered the crown to Raymond of St. Gilles, who refused, declaring that no man should be crowned king in the city were Christ lived and suffered. Robert Courte-Heuse was offered the crown next, but he also declined, for the same reason. Finally, Godfrey of Bouillon accepted "for the love of Christ" on July 22, although he refused to wear a crown through respect for Christ, who had been forced to wear the Crown of Thorns in that place. In fact, he never bore the actual title of king, instead taking the title *Advocatus Sancti Sepulchri* — Guardian of the Holy Sepulchre.

In spite of his pious refusal to accept the title, Godfrey was, for all practical purposes, the first Latin king of Jerusalem. There was little time, however, to rest on his laurels. Jerusalem may have fallen to the Christians, but it was not safe and, within a few months, Godfrey was required to lead his army against an Egyptian force sent to relieve the city. In addition, he led his men against numerous Muslim strongholds on the coast.

It is said that Godfrey remained true to his humbleness as a Christian in the Holy City, living in a tent with only a single cushion on which to rest. A legend with a more supernatural flavor has it that on the day of his election, the nobility went to church to pray, each holding a lighted candle. There was an earthquake and everyone was thrown to the ground; all the candles were extinguished except for Godfrey's.

Severin makes the wry but undoubtedly accurate comment that Godfrey's legendary status was immeasurably helped by the fact that he died soon after the conquest of Jerusalem. "Unlike other heroes such as King Arthur or the Cid who faded in their old age, re-emerging for one last burst of glory, the Duke made his exit while still at the height of his power." He died of a fever on July 18, 1100, and lay in state for five days before being buried at the foot of the Hill of Calvary. On his monument was this inscription:

Here lies the renowned Godfrey of Bouillon, who gained all this land for Christendom. May his soul rest in peace. Amen.

7

Warriors of Christ

The Knights Templar

In 1119, during the reign of Baldwin II, a knight of Champagne named Hugh of Payns and eight trusted companions bound themselves together in a perpetual vow to defend both the Holy Land and the safety of pilgrims traveling there. This knightly order, which began in abject poverty suffused with the light of piety and courage, would within two hundred years become one of the richest and most powerful organizations in the world. Its members would possess lands and riches beyond the wildest dreams of other mortals, together with a political and military potency to rival that of many nations. And yet, only a few years later, the Order of the Knights Templar would be utterly destroyed, its members tortured in the most horrible ways and burned at the stake amid rumors and accusations of devil worship, bestiality, human sacrifice, sodomy, and the desecration of religious objects.

The story of the order's remarkable rise and fall began in 1104, when Count Hugh of Champagne went on a pilgrimage to the Holy Land with a retinue of his knights. Hugh was the ruler of a large and wealthy principality that had been part of the West Frankish kingdom left by Charles the Bald. Among Count Hugh's knights was Hugh of Payns, a relation who served as an officer in the count's household and who possessed the benefice of Montigny. He was probably from the village whose name he bore, a few miles from Troyes on the Seine River, and from which Count Hugh ruled his lands.

It is not known with certainty whether Hugh of Payns accompanied Count Hugh on his first pilgrimage to Jerusalem, in 1104; however, he certainly accompanied him on his second, in 1114, and remained there when the count returned to Europe. Together with another knight, named Godfrey of St. Omer, Hugh of Payns approached King Baldwin II and Patriarch Warmund of Picquigny with a proposal to establish an order composed, essentially, of warrior-monks; men of piety and humility who were nevertheless merciless in the defense of the Christian Church against all enemies.

The king and the patriarch approved Hugh's plan, and on Christmas Day 1119, Hugh, together with eight others including Godfrey, Archambaud of St. Aignan, Payen of Montdidier, Geoffrey Bissot, and Roland, vowed to defend the Church of the Holy Sepulchre. Calling themselves the Poor Fellow-Soldiers of Jesus Christ, they kept the clothes of their knightly profession, chose the Mother of God as their patroness, and bound themselves to live according to the rules of St. Augustine. Hugh of Payns was elected their first leader.

In addition to providing them with several benefices, King Baldwin II gave them quarters in the former al-Aqsa Mosque, which he had converted into his palace and which stood on the southern edge of the Temple Mount, also known as the Temple of Solomon. Subsequently the order came to be known by several variations of the same name: the Poor Fellow-Soldiers of Jesus Christ and the Temple of Solomon, the Knights of the Temple of Solomon, the

Knights of the Temple, and the Templars. According to Piers Paul Read in his splendid history of the order, *The Templars:*

> It is possible that the original intention of Hugh of Payns and his companions was simply to withdraw into a monastery, or perhaps found a lay confraternity comparable to the hospice of Saint John that had been founded by the merchants of Amalfi to care for pilgrims before the First Crusade. Michael the Syrian, a medieval chronicler, suggested that it was King Baldwin, only too aware of his inability to police his kingdom, who persuaded Hugh of Payns and his companions to remain knights rather than become monks "in order to work to save his soul, and to guard these places against robbers." Another medieval historian of the crusades, James of Vitry, describes the dual nature of their commitment: "to defend pilgrims against brigands and rapists" but also to observe "poverty, chastity and obedience according to the rules of ordinary priests."

The Templars also took the vow to refrain from yielding even a foot of land to the enemy, and not to retreat, even if attacked in the proportion of three to one. In addition, their vow of poverty necessitated the sharing of one horse between two knights, which was later commemorated in the image on their seal (even when they became one of the wealthiest communities in the world).

In 1120, only one year after their establishment, a powerful French landowner, Fulk, count of Anjou, went on a pilgrimage to the Holy Land and enrolled as a married associate of the Templars. Much impressed with Hugh, Fulk endowed the order with an annual grant of thirty pounds of silver. This example was soon followed by many other devout European princes.

In 1125 Count Hugh of Champagne, with whom Hugh of Payns had first traveled to the Holy Land, returned, having repudiated his unfaithful wife and disinherited the son he believed was not his, to take the Templar vows. For the first nine years of its existence, the order maintained their vows of chastity and poverty, adopting a striped black and white banner called the *beauséant,* after their original piebald horse. They also continued to wear whatever clothes were donated to them.

King Baldwin II, realizing that the disunity among the Saracen enemies of Christianity could not last for long, and that they would, perhaps very soon, unite against the church in Outremer, decided that the Templars would be invaluable assets in the coming battles. In 1127 he sent Hugh of Payns, together with William of Bures, on a diplomatic mission to Western Europe. The intention was threefold: to persuade Fulk of Anjou to marry Baldwin's daughter Melisende and thus become heir to the throne of Jerusalem; to gather sufficient forces for a planned attack on Damascus; and to seek the official recognition by the pope of the Templars.

Hugh and William were granted an audience with St. Bernard of Clairvaux (1090?–1153), one of the handful of truly great men of the period. Born to a noble family, Bernard entered the Cistercian abbey of Citeaux at age twenty-two. Despite many opportunities to attain higher ecclesiastical office, he remained at the abbey all his life. A reputation for performing miraculous cures, coupled with a great erudition and eloquence, ensured that Bernard became the most influential religious figure in France and, ultimately, in Europe. He became an adviser to popes and was an indefatigable promoter of peace. Through his many writings, consisting of more than three hundred sermons, about five hundred known letters, and thirteen treatises, he greatly influenced the course of Roman Catholic spirituality. He was canonized in 1174, twenty-one years after his death.

Bernard was a great admirer of the Templars, saying of them:

> They go not headlong into battle, but with care and foresight, peacefully, as true children of Israel. But as

soon as the fight has begun, they rush without delay upon the foe . . . and know no fear . . . one has often put to flight a thousand; two, ten thousand . . . gentler than lambs and grimmer than lions; theirs is the mildness of monks and the valour of the knight.

At the end of January 1128 Hugh appeared before the Council of Troyes, an august gathering indeed, consisting of the archbishops of Rheims and Sens, ten bishops, and several abbots (including Bernard of Clairvaux), and presided over by the cardinal of Albano. The council decided that the Templars should receive papal recognition; and Pope Honorius II chose a plain white mantle for them. In 1146 Pope Eugenius III added a red cross.

Hugh's journey to Europe was phenomenally successful, in terms of both recruitment and the receiving of gifts and grants for their maintenance. King Henry I gave him a huge amount of gold and silver; and in Scotland, France, and Flanders armor and horses were donated.

In 1129 Hugh, together with three hundred other knights, led an enormous group of pilgrims to the Holy Land. Upon their arrival, King Baldwin II put into operation his plan to take Damascus. His army, which included a contingent of Templars, set out from the frontier fortress of Banyas in November and managed to get within six miles of Damascus before splitting up, with William of Bures taking a large body of men off to plunder. Almost immediately the group was attacked by Damascene cavalry and almost entirely wiped out. Baldwin intended to attack the enemy while they were busy celebrating this victory, but he was foiled by a sudden torrential downpour that flooded the roads and forced him to abandon his attempt on Damascus.

As Read states, over the next few years very little information is available on the activities of the Templars, and he suggests that during this time they were simply performing the duties for which the order had originally been formed: guarding the routes taken by pilgrims to the Holy Land.

During the Crusades, serious charges began to be leveled against the Knights Templar, including that they were actually fighting for no one but themselves. For example, in 1153 the Christians had besieged the city of Ascalon. The Templars were manning a large siege tower, to which the defenders of the city attempted to set fire; this they succeeded in doing, but the wind suddenly changed direction and blew the flames directly onto the city walls. The intense heat cracked the masonry, and part of the wall collapsed. According to the Latin chronicler William of Tyre, the Christian army was about to enter when the master of the temple, Bernard of Trémélay (Hugh of Payns died in 1136) claimed the right to take the city for himself and his men. The Templars plunged headlong into the breach but were cut to pieces by the defenders, and their headless bodies were hung from the walls. Although William claimed that the Templars were victims of their own greed, Piers Paul Read reminds us that recent research suggests the other knights simply failed to follow the Templars into the breach quickly enough, allowing them to be cut off. Whatever the true nature of events, this episode damaged the Templars' reputation.

One year after the fall of Ascalon, a Templar contingent ambushed an Egyptian force that was escorting Vizir Abbas and his son Nasir al-Din. The Templars killed Abbas and took his son prisoner, selling him into slavery to his enemies in Egypt, even though he had expressed the desire to convert to Christianity. He was subsequently sexually mutilated and tortured to death in Egypt.

By the fourteenth century the Templars had consolidated their authority and become one of the wealthiest and most powerful organizations in the world. Needless to say, their success provoked much envy, and their enemies began to grow in number. Throughout Europe they possessed churches, chapels, farms, villages, mills, pastures, fishing grounds, and forests. It has been estimated that the annual income of the order was about six million pounds sterling, an unbelievably large sum for the time.

At this point in its history, the order was composed of knights, chaplains, and serving brothers, as well as those who were merely affiliated to it, worked for it, or received its protection without taking the vows. According to Arkon Daraul in *A History of Secret Societies:*

> A candidate for knighthood should prove that he was of a knightly family and entitled to the distinction. His father must have been a knight, or eligible to become one. He had to prove that he was born in wedlock. The reason for this last requirement was said to be not only religious: there was the possibility that a political head such as a king or prince might influence the Order by managing to have one of his bastard sons enter it, later perhaps to rise to high rank therein, and finally attaching it to the service of his dominion.
>
> The candidate had to be unmarried and free from all obligations. He should have made no vow, nor entered any other Order; and he was not to be in debt. Eventually the competition for admission was so great from eligible people that a very high fee was exacted from those who were to be monk-warriors of the Temple.

The Templar initiation ceremony was highly secret, and this secrecy doubtless fueled the unsavory rumors regarding the order's practices. The master (or the prior, when the master was unavailable) began the initiation thus: "Beloved brethren, ye see that the majority are agreed to receive this man as a brother. If there be any among you who knows anything of him, on account of which he cannot lawfully become a brother, let him say it; for it is better that this should be signified beforehand than after he is brought before us."

If there was no objection, the prospective member was taken to another room with several Templar knights and coached on how to behave and make answers to the questions he would be asked. Following the giving of satisfactory answers, he was asked if he still desired to join the order. If he answered in the affirmative, another part of the ritual would commence, with more questions and answers regarding the candidate's willingness to devote himself utterly to the service of God and the brotherhood.

The principal architect of the Templars' downfall was Philip the Fair of France who, bankrupt, fearful and envious of the enormous power of the order, set in motion the wheels of rumor and conspiracy that would eventually see its members tortured and burned at the stake.

At this time Pope Clement V (a former archbishop of Bordeaux who had been made pope as a result of the machinations of Philip) wrote to both the Templars and the Hospitalers asking them to visit him for a conference, ostensibly to invite them to join a Crusade with the kings of Armenia and Cyprus. There had been much rivalry between the two orders, and he hoped that a reconciliation between them would strengthen his own position as their ultimate authority. William de Villaret, grand master of the Hospitalers, was engaging the Saracens of Rhodes at the time and thus could not accept the invitation. The grand master of the Templars, Jacques de Molay, accepted, and in the company of sixty Templar knights, sailed for France, taking with him 150,000 gold florins.

De Molay was received warmly by his enemy Philip. From Paris he journeyed to Poitiers, where he discussed the idea of a new Crusade with Pope Clement, maintaining that only an alliance of all Christendom (and not just between two religious orders) could defeat the Muslims. He also asked Clement to institute a papal commission to dispel the horrible rumors circulating about the Templars. The grand master then returned to the Paris Temple where, on the evening of October 12, 1307, he was arrested along with sixty of his fellow knights by Philip's troops.

Daraul summarizes the charges against the Templars thus:

1. Each Templar on his admission swore never to quit the Order, and to further its interests by right or wrong.
2. The heads of the Order are in secret alliance with the Saracens, and they have more of Mohammedan infidelity than Christian faith. Proof of the latter includes that they make every novice spit upon the cross and trample upon it, and blaspheme the faith of Christ in various ways.
3. The heads of the Order are heretical, cruel and sacrilegious men. Whenever any novice, on discovering the iniquity of the Order, tries to leave it, they kill him and bury the body secretly by night. They teach woman who are pregnant by them how to procure abortion, and secretly murder such newborn children.
4. They are infected with the errors of the Fratecelli; they despise the Pope and the authority of the Church; they scorn the sacraments, especially those of penance and confession. They pretend to comply with the rites of the Church simply to avoid detection.
5. The superiors are addicted to the most infamous excesses of debauchery. If anyone expresses his repugnance to this, he is punished by perpetual captivity.
6. The Temple-houses are the receptacle of every crime and abomination that can be committed.
7. The Order works to put the Holy Land into the hands of the Saracens, and favours them more than the Christians.
8. The Master is installed in secret and few of the younger brethren are present at this ceremony. It is strongly suspected that on this occasion he repudiates the Christian faith, or does something contrary to right.

9. Many statutes of the Order are unlawful, profane and contrary to Christianity. The members are therefore forbidden under pain of perpetual confinement to reveal them to anyone.

10. No vice or crime committed for the honour or benefit of the Order is held to be a sin.

In view of the forms of torture employed against the captured knights, it is hardly surprising that so many of them (123 of 138 interrogated) confessed to at least some of the charges leveled against them. These tortures were foul indeed, and included the rack, which was used to dislocate limbs; the thumbscrew; crushing with lead weights; wedges thrust under fingernails; and teeth ripped out, and the living nerves poked and prodded. As historian Desmond Seward states in his comprehensive study of the military religious orders *The Monks of War,* the Templars could have withstood such torments inflicted by their enemies the Muslims, but when the torturers were their fellow Christians they collapsed under the awful weight of starvation and despair.

Philip took possession of the Paris Temple and sent word to Edward II in England, recommending that he take action at once against the order there. Edward replied that he had serious doubts as to the veracity of the charges against the Templars, but Clement wrote assuring him that the grand master had himself confessed to the crime of denying Christ. Edward wrote to the kings of Portugal, Castile, Aragon, and Sicily, asking if there were any truth to the accusations. Although the replies he received maintained the Templars' innocence, Clement ordered Edward to use torture to extract confessions from the Templars imprisoned in England. Edward agreed, but ordered his torturers not to mutilate or to spill too much of the knights' blood.

In February 1312 the order was officially condemned; the following month Clement formally pronounced that the Templars were guilty of all charges, and in April the order was declared dissolved. Clement stated that although the Templars could not be convicted on the strength of the evidence against them, he believed them to be guilty. Their lands were given to their rivals the Hospitalers.

On March 14, 1314, the four Templar great officers, including Jacques de Molay, were paraded outside Notre Dame Cathedral to hear the sentence of life imprisonment that would be passed upon them. De Molay, who was nearly seventy, took this opportunity to voice his defiance and to proclaim his and the order's innocence one last time. Seward offers us his words:

> I think it only right that at so solemn a moment when my life has so little time to run I should reveal the deception which has been practised and speak up for the truth. Before heaven and earth and with all of you here as my witnesses, I admit that I am guilty of the grossest iniquity. But the iniquity is that I have lied in admitting the disgusting charges laid against the Order. I declare, and I must declare, that the Order is innocent. Its purity and saintliness is beyond question. I have indeed confessed that the Order is guilty, but I have done so only to save myself from terrible tortures by saying what my enemies wished me to say. Other knights who have retracted their confessions have been led to the stake; yet the thought of dying is not so awful that I shall confess to foul crimes which have never been committed. Life is offered to me but at the price of infamy. At such a price, life is not worth having. I do not grieve that I must die if life can be bought only by piling one lie upon another.

The following morning, along with his comrades, Jacques de Molay was taken to an island in the Seine River, and burned alive over a charcoal fire. According to legend, with his dying breath de Molay summoned both Philip and Clement to stand with him before God within one year.

Within one month, the pope was dead. Philip died that autumn.

The Knights Hospitalers

If the Knights Templar were the most enigmatic, romantic, and ultimately tragic order of the medieval period, the most important and long lasting must surely be the Hospitalers, or, more fully, the Order of the Hospital of St. John of Jerusalem. The order is said to have existed before the Crusades, and it survives even to the present day.

The man who founded the order is one of the most mysterious figures in history. All that is really known is that his name was Father Gerard; his birthplace and family name are now lost. That he was indeed the order's founder, however, is proven by a bull of Pope Paschal II dated 1113 and addressed to *"Geraudo institutori ac praeposito Hirosolimitani Xenodochii."* In 1100 Father Gerard had been elected master of the Hospital of St. John the Almoner for pilgrims at Jerusalem; the hospital had been founded in about 1070 by merchants from Amalfi. As the number of pilgrims steadily increased, Gerard abandoned the Benedictine rule for that of St. Augustine, and also adopted St. John the Baptist as patron.

Before the Crusades, there were many hospices (or *xenodochia*) in the Holy Land, belonging to different nations, that sheltered the pilgrims. The Italian hospice barely survived on alms gathered in Italy; however, the arrival of the Crusaders brought about a change in fortune, for they repaid Gerard's kindness and hospitality with territories and revenues, not only in the Kingdom of Jerusalem but also in Sicily, Italy, and Provence.

In 1120 Gerard was succeeded by Raymond of Provence, a brilliant administrator who enhanced the order's already considerable wealth and popularity. According to Desmond Seward:

Raymond was expert in providing an administration for these European possessions, setting up houses whose revenues were spent in forwarding food, wine, clothes and blankets for hospital use; some were specifically charged with providing luxuries, such as white bread, for the sick. The papacy gave the Hospitallers many privileges: Innocent II forbade bishops to interdict Hospitaller chapels; Anastasius IV gave them their own priests; and the English Adrian IV gave them their own churches.

In 1136 they received the first of their colossal fortresses, the castle of Gibelin, donated by King Fulk, on the road from Gaza to Hebron. Under the guidance of Father Raymond the Hospitalers took vows of poverty, chastity, and obedience, and wore a black mantle with a white cross on the chest. Their militarization was a slow process: in 1178 Pope Alexander III decreed that they should carry weapons only to defend the kingdom, or to attack a pagan city. At this point, the order's primary role was to care for the sick.

The order was divided into four classes: the knights of justice, who had to be of noble birth; sergeants; chaplains, who were charged with maintaining the spiritual well-being of the establishment; and serving brethren. In addition, there were honorary members, called *donats,* who contributed funds. At the height of their power they possessed more than twenty strongholds in Outremer and, according to one estimate, no fewer than nineteen thousand manors throughout Europe. They took part in the major campaigns of the Crusades, including the capture of Ascalon in 1154. When Jerusalem fell to Saladin and the Muslims in 1187, the order moved first to Margat and then to Acre, which they lost a little over a century later, in 1291. Under the command of their grand master, Jean de Villiers, they sought refuge in the Kingdom of Cyprus, where they already held a number of possessions.

On Cyprus the Hospitalers were welcomed by King Amaury,

who assigned to them as a place of residence the southern coastal town of Limassol. The geographic nature of their new headquarters obliged them to switch battle tactics, equipping fleets of ships to make war on the Muslims, and establishing themselves as the principal protectors of pilgrims traveling by sea to the Holy Land.

Cyprus, however, was a less than ideal location for a headquarters; so the Hospitalers turned their attention to Rhodes, which at that time was filled with Greek, Italian, and Saracen pirates who were causing serious problems for Christian trade throughout the region. The destruction of the Knights Templar, while benefiting the Hospitalers in many ways, had opened their eyes to the necessity of establishing a powerful stronghold, so in 1306 they sailed for the island under the command of Foulques de Villaret. Their forces amounted to two galleys and a handful of transport ships containing only thirty-five knights and five hundred infantry, plus two more galleys under the command of a Genoese adventurer named Vignole de' Vignoli.

Their first attempt to take the island failed, but in November they succeeded in storming the fortress of Philermo, and consolidated their victory by taking the city of Rhodes itself the following year. During their time on Rhodes, the Hospitalers became, essentially, a combination of sea knights and corsairs, battling against the piracy of the Saracens who were presenting such a serious danger to Christian merchantmen. The Hospitalers' response to this danger was twofold: to protect Christian commerce by attacking and giving chase to the pirate vessels; and also to make reprisals on the Turks, descending on and pillaging rich Turkish ports such as Smyrna, which they attacked in 1341.

During this period a new threat to Christianity presented itself in the form of the Ottoman Turks of Iconium. Following the fall of Constantinople, Mahomet II decided to consolidate and secure his gains by attacking the stronghold of Rhodes. This had the effect of forcing the order onto the defensive, and it lived with the perpetual fear of a catastrophic assault from the Saracens. Indeed, in the siege of 1480 under the command of Grand Master Pierre d'Aubusson, the order managed to throw off a full-scale Muslim assault on the island.

Forty-four years later the Muslims, under Sultan Suleiman II, descended again on the island with no fewer than four hundred ships and an army that was 140,000 strong. This time the knights endured as best they could, under Grand Master Philippe Villiers de l'Isle Adam; but eventually their supplies ran out and they were forced to capitulate. As an acknowledgment of the order's bravery, Suleiman II decided that their lives should be spared and that they should be allowed to return to Europe; he even lent them several ships for the journey.

Defeated but undaunted, the Hospitaler knights returned to their commanderies, and sent communications to Charles V, beseeching him to allow them to set up new headquarters on the island of Malta, which was a dependency of his kingdom of Sicily. The sovereignty of the island was granted to them in 1530.

The Hospitalers became known as the Knights of Malta for the next 268 years. As soon as they had established themselves on the island, they resumed the same activities as on Rhodes, fighting the Barbary pirates who were terrorizing the western Mediterranean. In spite of their small fleet of only seven galleys, they contributed greatly to Charles's expeditions against Tunis and Algiers. As might be expected, Suleiman II was less than pleased at the knights' activities, especially in view of his magnanimous treatment of them following the fall of Rhodes. So once again he moved his forces against them, and this culminated in the siege of Malta, which lasted for four months in 1565.

At this time part of the island had already fallen to the Turks. Half of the Knights of Malta and about eight thousand soldiers had fallen before a relief army arrived from Spain and delivered them. It is said that the Turks lost as many as thirty thousand men before they were forced to retreat. The new city of Valette was built on the ruins of the old one that had been destroyed by Suleiman's forces. It was not until the Battle of Lepanto in 1571, however, that the Ottoman threat was finally eliminated.

Afterward, the knights' presence on Malta was characterized chiefly by frequent, and small-scale, skirmishes with the Barbary corsairs who continued to harass the region. Although not terribly significant in historical terms, these engagements were of considerable importance to the young knights involved, for to achieve successes against the enemy could secure the knight a vacant commandery. It was still a time of extreme danger, with all the attendant risks of capture, and the financial ruin that would follow from paying ransoms; and yet the potential rewards were enormous for the captain with the intelligence and the courage to succeed.

One of the most lucrative trades was slavery. On one occasion several hundred Christian slaves, who had been kept as rowers on Turkish galleys, were liberated and their captors were themselves taken and sold as slaves on Christian galleys. In fact, Malta was an important slave market, with thousands of human beings bought and sold as commodities, many for use on the ships of the knights themselves. Historians have noted that in this climate of violence and awful brutality it is hardly surprising that the morality of the order itself should have degenerated, and that vicious infighting frequently broke out among the knights.

Even the grand masters were not safe from the ambitions of the other knights, and in 1581 Jean de la Cassière was made prisoner by his own men, who had taken great exception to his forbidding them to have relations with prostitutes. So much for their vow of celibacy. Likewise their vow of obedience to the grand master: when a knight secured possession of a commandery on the European mainland, he immediately considered himself quite independent of higher authority, and maintained relations with the rest of the order that were nominal, to say the least.

The vow of poverty also was ignored: knights were recruited

exclusively from the nobility, and the order's wealth was seen as the primary consideration in their activities. The order's material (as opposed to spiritual) decline began with its suppression in Protestant countries, or the appropriation of its commanderies to Protestant nobility, such as happened in Sonnenburg in Prussia. In Catholic countries the order came under attack from Catholic sovereigns who assumed the right to control the commanderies within their jurisdiction. Ultimately Malta itself was surrendered by the grand master, Count von Hompesch, to Napoleon Bonaparte during the latter's expedition to Egypt in 1798.

The order lost yet more property in Catholic countries following the French Revolution. However, respite came in the form of Czar Paul of Russia, who gave them numerous properties in his realm, in return for which he was elected grand master. His election was not recognized by the pope, however. From 1805 to 1879 the grand mastership was abolished, but was reinstated by Pope Leo XIII, who bestowed it on the Austrian Geschi di Sancta Croce.

In the twentieth century admission to the order depended on the Catholic faith, attainment of legal age, integrity of character, and high social position. The last four great priories were in Bohemia and Italy. The Order of the Knights of Malta owns the Convent of Santa Maria del Priorato on the Aventine in Rome. The convent contains many portraits of the knights, as well as an extensive archive of records regarding the order's history.

The order's property at Sonnenburg in Prussia was lost during the secularization of its property in 1810; however, in 1852 King Frederick William IV created a new confraternity known as the Johanitterorden, under a master who was always chosen from the royal family. Admission to this order is subject to various conditions, including ancient nobility and an entrance fee of nine hundred marks, followed by a four-year probationary period as a knight of honor before finally becoming a knight of justice. The main obligation of these knights is to collect contributions for hospitals; and so, like the Teutonic Knights, whom we shall meet next, the order has returned to the function for which it was first created.

The Teutonic Knights

The Teutonic Order was originally modeled on the Hospitalers and, like the latter, changed the location of its headquarters a number of times throughout its long history. Following the conquest of Jerusalem by Saladin in 1187, the Teutonic hospital for pilgrims from Germany, founded in Jerusalem in 1127, its church dedicated to the Virgin Mary, and its members known as Mariani, were broken up. During the Third Crusade, German merchants from Bremen and Lübeck, along with the duke of Holstein, established a temporary hospital by the besieged walls of Acre. These first headquarters consisted of nothing more than a large tent made from a ship's mainsail, in which their sick countrymen were received and cared for.

After the fall of Acre the hospital was permanently established within the city with the cooperation of Frederick of Swabia, leader of the German Crusade. In 1198 several noblemen joined the brethren, and a new military order was formed: the Teutonic Knights of St. Mary's Hospital of Jerusalem. A Rhinelander named Heinrich Walpot von Bassenheim was appointed master. Militarily, the order was run along lines similar to the Templars, and its hospital work was conducted after the manner of the Order of St. John.

There were three types of brother: knight, priest, and sergeant. The knights were required to be of noble birth and German blood, and wore a white cloak with a black cross; the priests wore a longer version of this garment, and the sergeants wore a gray cloak with a three-armed cross.

According to Desmond Seward in his superb history of the military religious orders *The Monks of War:*

The new brotherhood's hierarchy resembled that of the Poor Knights. Under the *Hochmeister* (*Magister Generalis*) were the *Gross-Komtur,* the *Ordensmarschall* (later called *Grossmarschall*), the *Spittler* (Hospitaller), the *Tressler* (Treasurer) and the *Trapier* (Quartermaster), who constituted the Grand Council. The General Chapter, which elected the Hochmeister, met every September on the feast of the Holy Cross. A commandery contained no fewer than twelve knight-brethren under a *pfleger* or *hauskomtur.* The houses of a province formed a *landkomturei* or *ballei*. In charge of German *balleien* was the *Landmeister* whose headquarters were at Mergentheim in Swabia.

The order received generous endowments from the empire, including lands in Germany, Sicily, and southern Italy. They concentrated their activities in Armenia, and their main strongholds were at Amouda and Haruniye. Their third hochmeister, Hermann Bart, led most of them to their deaths in a campaign in Cilicia in 1210. His successor was Hermann von Salza, whom Seward calls "the real founder of the Order's greatness." He was born in about 1170, and in his childhood attended the court of the dukes of Thuringia, where he acquired his gentle manners and developed his gift for diplomacy.

In 1219, following the siege of Damietta, at which the order had distinguished itself with its bravery, von Salza was awarded the privilege of wearing the gold cross of Jerusalem under the order's black cross. In 1226 Emperor Frederick II bestowed on him another reward, making him and his successors princes of the empire. In 1229 the Teutonic Knights were present at the coronation of the excommunicated Frederick as king of Jerusalem. In spite of this, von Salza remained on good terms with the papacy. That same year, another headquarters was constructed northeast of Acre, to defend the thin corridor of land connecting Jerusalem with the sea.

The Teutonic Knights' most significant contribution to history lay not in the Holy Land, however, but in the Baltic region, whose pagan tribes had hitherto resisted the efforts of missionaries, many of whom had been killed. To avenge their deaths, a Crusade was proclaimed. Albrecht von Bux-hövden, who had founded the town of Riga at the mouth of the Dvina River, and who later became its bishop, founded an order called the Sword Brethren, which was modeled on the Knights Templar. Albrecht's intention was not only to convert the heathen populations of this region but also to colonize it. The Sword Brethren built the castle of Wenden as a headquarters, and then invaded Estonia and the island of Oesel, which contained a shrine to the pagan god Tarapilla.

At this time a savage pagan people called the Prusiskai provided Hermann von Salza with what he saw as an ideal training opportunity for his order. These heathens lived along the seaboard from the Vistula to the Niemen and in the inland areas, which were covered with pine forests, lakes, and marshes. They were a truly terrifying and formidable people, and Seward's description of them is well worth quoting here:

> Balts worshipped idols in sacred groves and fields, and attributed divine powers to the entire creature-world, including their own animals. They practised human sacrifice, by burning or beheading, and buried animals alive at funerals; dead warriors were cremated astride their horses, while widows were often made to hang themselves. Stockades of towns and temples were adorned with animal skulls to ward off the evil eye, their grim shrines served by weird priests and soothsayers. The Prussians' domestic habits were as unpleasant as their religion. The old, the sick, the blind and the lame were invariably slaughtered. Drunkenness from mead and fermented mares' milk was a major pastime while tribesmen often drank the living blood from their horses' veins. Inter-tribal warfare was endemic.

So frequent and violent were the heathen raids into Poland that a duke named Konrad of Mazovia decided to ask for the assistance of the Teutonic Knights, offering them in return the province of Chelmo, which he had been forced to abandon, and whatever else they could seize from the pagans. In 1223 von Salza was given sovereignty over these lands by the emperor in a document known as the Golden Bull of Rimini, which was later confirmed by Pope Honorius III. The following year saw the arrival of a knight called Hermann Balke, who was to become one of the order's great heroes. In the company of twenty-eight of his brother knights and an army of German Crusaders, he began a struggle for supremacy over the pagans that lasted twenty-five years.

Balke was an extremely skillful warrior and made excellent use of aid from Silesia, Bohemia, and Lübeck. One of his first acts was to cross the Vistula and storm a pagan fortress-temple, hanging a Prussian chief from a sacred oak tree. The battles that followed must have presented a strange and terrifying sight, with the Crusader knights adopting the Prussian tactic of forest ambush, and descending on their enemies in their white robes, which gave excellent camouflage against the snow-covered landscape. In the evocative words of the German historian Treitschke: "Often under the weird glitter of the Northern Lights combat was joined upon the ice that covered the rivers and marshes, until the solid crust broke beneath the weight of the warriors and the men of both sides were engulfed to their chilly doom."

The pagans were no match for the Teutonic Knights, who employed hurling engines to demolish the Prussians' primitive forts. Balke also took advantage of the intertribal strife by allying himself with one tribe against another. Those tribes who converted to Christianity were spared the sword and allowed to keep their lands.

In 1232 the town of Kulm was founded on the Vistula, and the following year a Northern Crusade was proclaimed, which saw fifteen hundred Prussians killed. In 1235 the Teutonic Order was united with the much smaller and lesser-known Order of Dobrzyn, and two years later the town of Elbing was founded near the mouth of the Vistula, which allowed the knights to attack their enemies along the Baltic Sea promontory known as the Frisches Haff. Having routed their heathen enemies from the region, the knights now created their order-state, into which German colonists comprising all levels of society were brought.

In 1309 the fifteenth grand master, Sigfried of Feuchtwangen, transferred his residence from Venice, where at that time the knights had their chief house, to the Castle of Marienburg, which became the symbol of the Teutonic Order and which Seward describes as "a combination of fortress, palace, barracks and monastery."

Although the number of knights in the order never exceeded a thousand, it ruled its country along military lines and, with the more or less constant arrival of new Crusaders from other parts, it was able to dominate the region against the pagans, which included the inhabitants of Lithuania. In the Battle of Rudau in 1307 the Lithuanians were vanquished, and several decades later were converted to Christianity when their grand duke Jagellon married the heiress to the Kingdom of Poland in 1386.

This effectively ended paganism in this part of Europe, and with it the greatest period of the order's history. There followed a time of intense and continuous conflicts with the kings of Poland. They were defeated in 1410 in a battle between Tannenberg and the nearby village of Grünwald, which saw Polish and Lithuanian forces under Jagellon halting the eastward expansion of the Teutonic Knights. This defeat cost the Teutonic Knights eighteen thousand men, including six hundred knights, and decimated their finances. In an effort to swell their diminished coffers, the order resorted to increasing taxation throughout their lands, which aroused the native nobility. Another war resulted in the order losing half of its territory and being forced to give over the remainder to the suzerainty of the king of Poland in 1466.

The grand master's residence was transferred from Marienburg to Königsberg. To protect itself against the Polish kings, the order found it necessary to rely on Germany and to give the office of grand master to German princes. However, in 1511 Albert of Brandenburg embraced Lutheranism and made Prussia a fief of his house. Dignitaries in the rest of Germany broke with this apostate and chose a new grand master, Walter of Cronenberg, who established his residence at Mergentheim in Franconia in 1526.

The loss of Prussia began a series of losses of the Teutonic Knights' possessions throughout northern Europe, culminating in 1580 with the secession of Utrecht in the Low Countries. Louis XIV took most of its possessions in France, and the Treaty of Lunéville in 1801 relieved it of its possessions on the left bank of the Rhine. Thus, by the early nineteenth century, the Teutonic Order was left only with possessions in the Tyrol and the Austrian states.

At this stage the order came under the authority of the Austrian emperor, who reserved the office of grand master for an archduke of his own house. Besides this Catholic branch there was (and is) a Protestant branch in Utrecht, whose members had to profess the Calvinist religion. When Napoleon took possession of Holland in 1811, he suppressed the order, but this was reversed in 1815.

In the present day there are some twenty knights who are bound by an oath of celibacy, and thirty knights of honor who are not celibate but who must pay an annual contribution. The order's revenues are set aside for religious works. It has charge over parishes, schools, and hospitals, and performs ambulance service during wartime. Indeed, after nearly a millennium of existence, the Teutonic Knights perform the function for which they were first created: to serve as hospitalers.

The Knights of Calatrava

This illustrious order was founded in Castile during the re-conquest of Spain in the twelfth century as a military branch of the Cistercians. The Cistercian Order, which had been formed in 1098, contained many monks who had previously been knights; with the Order of Calatrava, the opposite was the case: those who had once been monks now served as knights. The story of the order was originally told by a man named Rodrigo of Toledo, and in it we see how the Calatrava knights epitomized that special group of men whom Desmond Seward famously called "the monks of war."

Calatrava (Qalat Rawaah, The Castle of War) is the Arabic name of a fortress sixty-five miles south of Toledo on the banks of the Guardiana River in south-central Spain. It was recovered from the Muslims in 1147 by the Emperor Alfonso VII, who well understood that to keep the castle would be far more difficult than taking it had been. The king turned to the Knights Templar for help in holding Calatrava: after all, they had vowed to wage perpetual war against the Muslims. The Templars attempted to make good their word, but in the face of formidable Muslim patrols in the region, decided that the castle could not be held, and abandoned it in 1157.

At that time a Cistercian abbot named Ramón Sierra, from the Navarrese monastery of Santa María de Fitero, was in Toledo in the company of a monk, Diego Velásquez, who was a nobleman and a friend of the king of Castile, Sancho III. Ramón requested an audience with the king, at which he offered to protect Calatrava. The idea was probably suggested to him by Diego, who had been a knight and thus was well versed in taking and defending castles. Their fighting force would come from the Cistercian lay brotherhood, who were variously employed as herdsmen and laborers.

The king agreed, and in 1158 the castle and its lands were given to the men of Fitero. Ramón took all his monks to the castle, where they were joined by a large number of Navarrese soldiers. An entirely new military order was thus created, which took its name from the castle given to it by the king. Once they had been fully equipped the brethren were ready to defend the castle; but for six years no attack came. When Ramón died in 1164 the monks elected a new leader, Don García. The choir monks left the castle at this time, to live at the monastery of Cirvelos. Velásquez and a few other clerics, acting as chaplains, remained in Calatrava with the knights. In the same year, Pope Alexander III issued a bull giving them canonical status as a religious order.

In 1187 the Order of Calatrava was given its definitive rule, which was approved by Pope Gregory VIII. Based on the Cistercian rule, it imposed on the knights not only their religious vows but also the rule of silence in the refectory, dormitory, and oratory; abstinence on four days of the week; several fast days during the year; to recite a certain number of Paternosters each day; to sleep in their armor; and to wear the Cistercian white mantle with the scarlet cross. Calatrava was obedient to Morimond in Burgundy, which was the motherhouse of Fitero, so the abbot of Morimond retained the right to visit the order and to alter its statutes. According to Seward:

A chapter general was held at Calatrava, at Christmas, Easter and Pentecost, when all *caballeros* [knights] were bound to attend and receive the sacraments. Each commandery was inspected annually by a knight and a chaplain to ensure that the rule was kept and fortifications maintained. These commanderies, manned by twelve experienced *freyles* [brothers], served as a blockhouse for their district, all able-bodied fighting men rallying to the commander in times of danger. In 1179 a commandery was founded in Aragon, at Alcañiz, to fight the Moors of Valencia. This became one of the Order's great houses, with many chaplains, and its conventual life resembled that at Calatrava.

The order's initial success, however, was followed by disaster. The Moors of Spain had no intention of abandoning their lost dominions, so they looked to the Moors of Africa for aid. This resulted in the invasion of the Almohads (unitarians), who saw holy war as their religious duty. In 1194 King Alfonso VIII of Castile issued a challenge to Caliph Yakub ibn-Yusuf to come to Spain and do battle. This he did the following year, entering the country with an enormous army. Alfonso made a grievous error, however, in boasting that his Castilian knights would be able to vanquish the enemy alone. On hearing this the kings of León and Navarre did not join him, and he was left to face the Moors with only the Orders of Calatrava and Santiago; as such, he was hopelessly outnumbered.

Seward describes the arms and armor of each side thus:

Spanish weapons and armour were those used throughout Europe: sword and lance, steel helmet, chain tunic and shield. Tactics were based on the single, decisive charge, though there was a tendency to wear lighter equipment and ride Arab horses. Auxiliary cavalry had little more than a lance, javelins and a knife. Infantry consisted of spearmen, slingers and archers carrying swords or axes. A rich man's arms were often jewelled and damascened in the Saracen fashion, especially the superb swords from Toledo, while Andalusian mantles were worn and some knights preferred to use Moorish scimitars.

Almohad cavalry, Berber or Andalusian, wore mail shirts and spiked onion helmets, charging with spears held overarm or hurling javelins. Their swords were light scimitars, their shields heart-shaped, their armour often gilded or silvered, and they used lassos or hooked lances to pull opponents from the saddle. The infantry were usually Negroes with broad-bladed stabbing spears and enormous hide shields, supported by archers and slingers who could discharge lethal clay bullets from a surprising distance. Moorish horsemen frequently swamped Spanish cavalry by sheer numbers, preventing them from choosing suitable ground for assembling their elaborate formations. If the Christians did manage to launch a charge, its impact was often absorbed by a dense mass of infantry sometimes roped together.

The two armies met on July 18, 1195, outside the Moorish castle of Alarcos near Ciudad Real. In spite of their great heroism the Spanish forces were utterly destroyed, with twenty-five thousand killed or taken prisoner. Some managed to escape to the commandery of Guadalherza, which they managed to hold against the pursuing Berbers, while another group tried to make a stand in a pass near La Zarzuela. They were far less fortunate: the enemy descended on them, and they were all massacred. Yakub was not satisfied with Alarcos, however; over the next two years he advanced steadily north, taking Guadalajara, Madrid, Uclés, and Calatrava, where he put the chaplains to death and turned the chapel into a mosque.

What was left of the Order of Calatrava found refuge in the Cistercian monastery of Cirvelos; and from there they began to organize their revival through the recruitment of new knights. With their numbers suitably bolstered, they felt able to take up arms once again against the Muslims. After a victory at the Castilian stronghold of Salvatierra in 1198, they took that name, becoming the Knights of Salvatierra for the next fourteen years. However, this good fortune was not to last, for the Almohads launched a fresh assault against Salvatierra and, in spite of the knights' valiant defense, took it.

The fall of Salvatierra sent shock waves through Spain and the rest of Europe, and prompted Pope Innocent III to make a plea to all Crusaders to go to the aid of the Spanish knights. The year 1212 saw the retaking of Calatrava itself by the Christians, in addition to the epic battle at Las Navas de

8

Tolosa, seventy miles east of Alarcos, which saw the Christians vanquish an enormous Muslim army.

In 1216 the knights returned to their former stronghold, took the name of Calatrava once again, and their influence spread throughout the Iberian peninsula. They were joined by other orders, such as Alcántara in the Kingdom of León and Avis in the Kingdom of Portugal. The year 1229 saw the coalition of Castile and León under King Ferdinand the Saint, followed six years later by the conquest of the Muslim capital city, Cordova, and then the surrender of the strongholds of Murcia, Jaen, and Seville. In spite of these successes the Moors managed to retain their Kingdom of Granada in the south for two more centuries, during which time it presented a constant danger as the Moorish point of entry into Europe.

The Order of Calatrava became a considerable force throughout Spain, possessing vast lands and castles, and exercising feudal lordship over thousands of vassals. It was also independent in temporal terms (i.e., on Earth), and in spiritual terms its only superiors were the abbot of Morimond and the pope. With this enormous affluence and power came the perhaps inevitable decline into intrigue and cold ambition, as exemplified by the schism that occurred in 1296 through the election of two grand masters, García Lopez and Gautier Perez. Following his dispossession by a delegate of Morimond, Lopez appealed to Pope Boniface VIII, who reversed the decision. However, following a quarrel with his lieutenant, Juan Nuñez, Lopez voluntarily resigned as grand master in favor of Nuñez, on the condition that he, Lopez, should be allowed to retain the commandery of Zurita. When this condition was violated, he again took the title of grand master in Aragon.

A serious conflict between the crown and the order broke out with the accession of Pedro the Cruel (1334–1369) in 1350. When he deserted his wife, Blanche of Bourbon, for María Padilla and bestowed inordinate favors on her family, he aroused the anger of the nobility. There were several rebellions fomented by Pedro's illegitimate half brother Enrique of Trastámara, which Pedro violently suppressed. He had three grand masters of the Order of Calatrava put to death: the first, charged with being in league with the king of Aragon, was beheaded in 1355; he himself killed the second, Estevañez, in the royal palace for having competed for the grand mastership with García de Padilla (María's brother); and the third was García himself, for having switched his loyalty from Pedro to Enrique of Trastámara.

Later, in 1366, with the help of Aragon and France, Enrique invaded Castile and forced Pedro to flee. He was crowned King Enrique II of Castile at Burgos in the same year. Four years earlier, however, Pedro had allied himself with England and, with the help of Edward the Black Prince, defeated Enrique and the French commander Du Guesclin at Nájera in 1367. Enrique then raised a new army with Du Guesclin and defeated and killed Pedro at Montiel in 1369.

As with other military orders, the struggle against the Turks, which had been the reason for the Calatrava Order's creation, became almost incidental to its other activities, which revolved around various political conflicts. Also in common with other orders, the knights of Calatrava descended to internecine conflicts, with various internal factions battling each other for power and influence. Royal authority began to impinge on the process of electing the grand master, whose station ensured a comparable degree of power, as in 1404, when Enrique of Villena was elected twenty-fourth grand master. Enrique was married and unfamiliar with the order, and was granted the position only through the favor of Enrique III of Castile. This created a schism within the order that was not healed until the king's death in 1414, when the election of Villena was canceled in favor of his rival, Luís Guzmán.

When Guzmán died in 1442 a new schism arose when King Juan II of Castile succeeded in forcing on the electors his own candidate, a bastard named Alfons of Aragon. Alfons, however, betrayed the king by joining a group opposing him, so Juan attempted to have him deposed. On this occasion a division among the electors resulted in three potential grand masters: Alfons in Aragon; Juan Ramírez de Guzmán, who was supported by the commanderies in Andalusia; and a new contender, Pedro Girón.

Following the withdrawal of his rivals, Pedro Girón became grand master in 1457. Belonging to a powerful Castilian family, Pedro was wily and ambitious, a schemer who had his own family's interests at heart, rather than those of the order. He supported Enrique IV against Juan II, and then Alfons (who had designs on the throne itself) against Enrique IV. Enrique was well aware of the power Pedro wielded, and in an attempt to ensure his loyalty, he offered him the hand in marriage of his sister Isabella of Castile. He took up this offer (his own vow of celibacy already having been annulled by Pope Pius II) and set out for Madrid, escorted by a powerful body of knights. During the journey he stopped to rest at a castle, and was alarmed to see a flock of white storks hovering in the air above. The next day he went to bed with an acute inflammation of the tonsils and died three days later.

At the height of its power and prosperity, the Order of Calatrava controlled fifty-six commanderies and sixteen priories distributed between the Diocese of Jaén and the Vicariate of Ciudad Real. Among its lordships were sixty-four villages, and the two hundred thousand people who lived in them generated an annual income for the order of approximately fifty thousand ducats. Such affluence could not but excite the jealousy of the monarchs, in addition to the suspicion they felt toward such a powerful and autonomous organization.

The opinion of Calatrava was of immense importance in the struggle between Alfonso V of Portugal and Ferdinand of Aragon. In 1458 Alfonso reignited the Holy War in North Africa. He sent an expedition of twenty-five thousand men, including knights from all orders, which captured the strategically important town of Alcacer-Sehgir. Between 1463 and 1464 Tangier was attacked three times, and many mountain villages also were raided. Tangier fell in 1471, and Afonso declared himself "King of Portugal and the Algarves on this side and beyond the sea in Africa."

The Knights of Calatrava were once again divided, this time between Afonso and Ferdinand, Grand Master Rodrigo Girón favoring Portugal, and his lieutenant, López de Padilla, supporting Aragon. This schism, the last in the history of the order, was eliminated at the Battle of Toro in 1476, which saw the annihilation of the Portuguese and the establishment of Ferdinand as king of Aragon in 1479.

In 1482 Rodrigo Girón was killed in the war against the Moors, at the siege of Loja, and was succeeded by López de Padilla. He was the last of the twenty-seven independent grand masters of the order, and his tenure was distinguished by a brief return to the piety and virtue of earlier times. This period reached its zenith with the reconquest of Granada from the Moors, although Padilla did not live to see it.

In 1476 the sultan of Granada, Muley Hassan, refused to pay tribute to Castile, provocatively informing the Castilian ambassador that Granadine mints no longer coined gold, only steel. Five years later, in 1481, the Moors attacked the frontier town of Zahara and massacred most of its population. Isabella sent the master of Calatrava to Jaén, and the master of the Order of Santiago to Écija to reinforce the garrisons.

Early the following year a Castilian force stormed the town of Alhama. When Muley Hassan heard of this, he was so enraged that he killed the messenger who had brought him the news. He made several attempts to recapture the town but was unsuccessful, and was further infuriated when the Christians threw the rotting corpses of Moors over the city walls, where they were eaten by dogs.

Following his vain attempts to retake Alhama, Hassan, who was an old man, returned to Granada to find that his son, Abu Abdullah, had been proclaimed sultan in his absence. He had no choice but to take refuge with his brother, az-Zagal, at Málaga.

Ferdinand, on the other hand, was filled with encouragement and decided to throw his forces against the city of Loja. The *cadi*, Ali-Atar, surrounded them with his own men and forced them to take refuge in a ravine, where Moorish horsemen mounted frequent attacks and slew many, taking their heads as saddle ornaments. The Castilian force barely managed to retreat.

Undaunted, Ferdinand and Isabella hired mercenaries from all over Europe, who brought with them cannons, siege engines, and many other weapons. The gunners came from Germany and Italy; from France came Crusader knights; and from England came archers who had recently fought in the Wars of the Roses. The targets for these new forces were the three main cities of the Kingdom of Granada: Málaga in the west; Almería in the east; and the capital, Granada. Seward writes:

> Captured towns became bridgeheads, garrisoned during the winter, so that no ground had been lost when the advance was resumed the following spring. Light troops systematically devastated the [tilled land] on a scale hitherto unknown, while the Castilian and Catalan fleets blockaded the coast, their war-galleys chasing Barbary merchantmen away from Granadine ports.

The fall of the city of Ronda in 1485 was the beginning of the end of Moorish rule in Granada. With the surrender of Málaga and the arrival of Queen Isabella, who built the city of Santa Fé (Holy Faith) opposite the capital, the Christian victory over the Moorish occupiers was complete, as was the Reconquista.

The political autonomy of the Order of Calatrava ended following the death of Padilla in 1487. Ferdinand, wishing to control the military orders rather than destroy them, secured a bull from Pope Innocent VIII investing him with the authority to administer them. Likewise, the canonical bond between Calatrava and its motherhouse of Morimond in Burgundy was weakened by Ferdinand's reluctance to allow foreign intervention in the affairs of Spain. Eventually, in 1630, it was decided that Morimond should be allowed to elect the grand prior but that its choice should be limited to Spanish Cistercians.

In 1652, under Philip IV, the order took a new vow to defend the doctrine of the Immaculate Conception. From then on, the order became almost completely inactive, and its possessions were finally dissipated in the general secularization of 1838. The Order of Calatrava still exists, however, along with the three other Spanish orders of Santiago, Alcántara, and Montesa. The grand master is King Juan Carlos.

8

Mercenaries

The Catalan Company

During the eleventh century there developed a type of soldier who fought not for his lord or his country, but rather for personal profit. It is probable that the Catalan Company was the first true company of mercenaries in Western Europe. Originally raised in 1281 to fight in the War of the Sicilian Vespers, in which the Angevin and Aragonese dynasties fought bitterly over control of the Kingdom of Sicily, the company distinguished itself as a powerful fighting force. The company was made up partly of Almogavars and Aragonese, who had previously been engaged in the Spanish Reconquista. By the time the war had ended twenty years later, the Catalan Company was under the command of Roger de Flor, a former pirate and sergeant in the Knights Templar who had become rich during the fall of Acre in 1291 using a Templar galley to ferry fugitives from Acre to Cyprus for huge sums.

When the war ended with the peace of Caltabellota in 1302, the six-thousand-strong Catalan Company was no longer needed, and the island's people desperately wanted them to leave, for as we have seen, demobilized mercenaries could and did wreak havoc in village and countryside. They next took service with the Byzantine emperor Andronikos II against the advancing Turks, conducting a campaign of brutal raids through the Turkish-held lands in Byzantine Nicaea. In the meantime, they had recruited some three thousand Turkic horsemen, and soon came to be considered by the Byzantines to be little more than violent and uncontrollable brigands. The military successes enjoyed by the Catalans during this time exacerbated de Flor's already arrogant temperament, and he began to make plans to establish his own version of the Byzantine Empire in Anatolia. These plans did not sit very well with the emperor, who ordered de Flor's assassination, following which many of the Catalan Company were massacred.

Command of the company then passed to Ramon Muntaner, who led it to victory against Byzantine forces at Apros in 1305 before proceeding to Rhaidestos, which became their new headquarters for raids throughout Thrace for the next two years. However, dissension grew within their ranks, and this, combined with powerful Byzantine resistance to their raids, forced them to move their headquarters to Thessaly in northern Greece, from which they targeted their raids on the Eastern Orthodox monasteries of Mount Athos.

In 1310 the Catalan Company found itself a new employer in Walter of Brienne, the duke of Athens and one of the leaders of the Romanian Frankish Latin Empire. They performed astonishingly well, capturing some thirty castles for him. However, when Walter foolishly attempted to dismiss them without pay, they turned the full force of their fury against him, and defeated him in a battle at Kephissos. The strategy they used was simple and brilliant, although it was based on what in modern parlance would be called a "dirty trick." On the day in question, the Catalan forces stood arrayed for battle behind a field that, unknown to Walter and his men, had recently been flooded. When the duke of Athens gave the order to charge, his forces were immediately trapped in the waterlogged ground, and were slain with ease by the Catalans. With that, the duke's principality came under the company's control, and they were able to hold it successfully for nearly eighty years, until another Spanish company, the Navarrese, set its sights on the Duchy of Athens and attacked it together with a Florentine force.

The Catalan Company was defeated in 1388 at Anastasioupolis, on the road between Xanthi and Komotini. This defeat, and the loss of their possessions, spelled the end for the Catalan Company, and it broke apart soon afterward.

Sir John Hawkwood and Mercenary Warfare in Italy

Italy in the fourteenth century was undergoing a transition in which imperial power was declining in the face of the growing power of the city-states. Not only did these miniature states vie with each other for power, but also with large states such as France and Aragon. For this reason the soldiers of fortune (or *condottieri*) found themselves much in demand. Some of them were nobles, some were commoners whose skill and bravery carried them up through the ranks, but all were driven by a lust for the money that could be gained from ransoming prisoners or descending like carrion birds upon an ill-defended town or city. While success could make them fortunes, poor performance could just as easily see them replaced by talented newcomers, of whom there was never any shortage. Like modern celebrities, they often took full advantage of their swashbuckling reputations. Bradbury quotes an amusing little chant about a mercenary named Niccolo d'Este:

On this side and that of the Po
All are the children of Niccolo.

In Italy as elsewhere in Europe besiegers could be incredibly ruthless in their treatment of a town and its inhabitants. For example, the brave and colorful countess of Forli, mother of Giovanni de Medici, commanded the citadel following the assassination of her husband, Girolamo Riario. Her children were captured and paraded before her by the besiegers, who threatened to kill them if she did not surrender. The countess, however, displayed a quite incredible intransigence in the face of this horrible threat: lifting up her skirts, she shouted at the besiegers that they were fools if they did not realize how easily she could make more children. In the event, the besiegers were unable to carry out their threat: the citadel was rescued by the countess's relatives, members of the powerful Sforza family.

Later, during her conflict with Cesare Borgia, she was besieged again, and this time looked down on her enemies wearing plate armor. When the attacking force broke through her defenses, she retired to her citadel and attempted to blow herself up with gunpowder before being captured. Bradbury notes how her son Giovanni became a leader of considerable audacity:

> At one council when a discussion was held about how to take a particular place, Giovanni became so impatient with the drawn-out arguments, which seemed to be ignoring his professional advice, that he advanced on the town and took it, then returned to find the meeting still in progress! It was the son of this Giovanni Medici who was to become the ruler of Florence.

From the general bloody and chaotic melee of medieval mercenary warfare there occasionally arose a commander who achieved legendary status. One such was Sir John Hawkwood, known in Italy as Giovanni Acuto, one of the finest generals of the medieval period. Hawkwood was born in about 1320 at Sible Hadingham near Colchester, Essex, England, the second son of Gilbert Hawkwood, a minor landowner and tanner. With an inheritance amounting to twenty pounds sterling and some corn, Hawkwood decided to join the army of Edward III, achieving knighthood and the command of a company by 1360.

Following the Peace of Brétigny between England and France that year, Hawkwood, in common with many other soldiers, found himself without a job. With little money and few prospects, he eventually joined one of the free companies of mercenaries who were causing havoc in various parts of Europe at the time, such as the Great Company of the German Werner von Urslingen, on whose breastplate was inscribed this terrifying epithet: "Enemy of God, Enemy of Piety, Enemy of Pity." Hawkwood joined the Great Company of the Marquis of Montferrat along with a troupe of his own men, composed of Englishmen and Gascons.

One of the most prominent and famous of the free companies was the White Company, with which Hawkwood went to war against the lords of Milan in 1360. In return for their service, the White Company received 60,000 francs from the lords of Florence, 10,000 of which Hawkwood kept for himself. The White Company then split into two, with some men going to Spain and the rest remaining in Italy under Hawkwood's command. Although his men were violent and unpredictable mercenaries, they were extremely loyal to him, staying with him even after defeats. The reason for this seems straightforward enough: he took good care of his men and always ensured that they were paid fairly and on time. Although scrupulously fair when dealing with his own men, he could nevertheless be bribed, on one occasion taking 130,000 florins from the city of Florence not to engage it in combat for five years. Other towns offered him 95,000 florins, plus 1,200 florins per year for life, which gives some idea of the awe in which he was held. In 1377 Hawkwood married Donnina, the illegitimate daughter of Bernarbo Visconti, gaining himself a castle, villa, and land in the bargain.

While Hawkwood was renowned for conducting his battles on foot, taking advantage of the speed and accuracy of archers and foot soldiers, it is also likely that he was the first to use artillery in Italy, at the Battle of Castagnaro in 1387. He commanded a Paduan army of 7,000 mounted soldiers, 1,000 infantry, and 600 English archers. The army of Verona against which he marched was composed of 9,000 cavalry and 2,600 infantry and pikemen (see "The Pikemen of Switzerland" later in this chapter). Hawkwood's army defeated the Veronese after outflanking them, and captured some 5,400 soldiers; 716 were killed and 846 wounded — and all this with a loss of just 100 Paduan soldiers.

One of the most highly regarded and feared soldiers of the time, John Hawkwood remained loyal to Florence in the last years of his life, and was rewarded with a salary until his death, which came to him in 1394 as he was selling his Italian estates and preparing to return to England. He was sixty-eight. In recognition of his martial contribution the Florentines gave him a state funeral, and in 1436 the artist Paolo Ucello painted a marvelous fresco of the knight in the Duomo in Florence.

The Pikemen of Switzerland

According to the historian Michael Mallett, "the mercenaries par excellence of the second half of the fifteenth century were the Swiss pikemen and their later imitators, the south German *Landsknechte.*" They had been known for many years to possess great prowess with the pike and halberd, but it was not until the early fourteenth century that these tough and resilient peasants finally came into their own, offering their services as mercenaries to towns such as Zurich. Victories gained over formidable foes, such as the Austrian cavalry at Sempach in 1386, enhanced their reputation as a military force to be reckoned with; and by the early 1400s the Diet of the Swiss Confederation began to receive requests for pike-men from all over Europe.

Their ascendancy reached its peak, however, with their defeat of Charles the Bold's forces at Granson (1476), Morat (1476), and Nancy (1477). Charles the Bold (1433–1477), last reigning duke of Burgundy (1467–1477), was the son and successor of Philip the Good. As the count of Charolais, Charles opposed the power of King Louis XI and had Louis arrested during a meeting at Péronne. In 1468 he married Margaret, the sister of King Edward IV, thus allying himself with England. He ruled Burgundy, Flanders, Artois, Brabant, Luxembourg, Holland, Zeeland, Friesland, and Hainault; but to achieve his dream of reestablishing the Kingdom of Lotharingia, he also needed Alsace and Lorraine. With this goal in mind he embarked on negotiations with Holy Roman emperor Frederick III to arrange the marriage of his daughter Mary to the emperor's son Maximilian. The marriage did take place, but only after Charles's death at the Battle of Nancy. Charles was undone by his desire to conquer the lands separating his possessions, which led to war with the Swiss.

The three famous battles mentioned above demonstrated the importance of the Swiss pike phalanx and close-quarter charging. The Swiss were highly mobile and agile, their armor consisting only of a breastplate and helmet. When cavalry was deployed against them, their pikes prevailed; even the artillery of the time was too heavy and difficult to maneuver to be of any significant use. Following these battles, it became clear to every ruler in Europe that Swiss pike infantry was an essential military element.

The use of mercenaries was cause for heated debate in the Europe of the late fifteenth century. According to Michael Mallett: "On the one side, Italian humanists deplored the use of hired soldiers to defend states which should have been developing their own military potential." Niccolò Machiavelli was convinced that the best armies had effective infantry at their core, and that these men should not be mercenaries fighting for the highest bidder, but rather citizens defending their own lands and homes. As Mallett points out, however, Machiavelli ignored the fact that the Swiss pikemen, who at that time were by far the best infantry in Europe, were themselves mercenaries.

Conclusion

From Lance to Firearm

Advances in weapons technology during the later Middle Ages gradually made the knight's position as the most significant single element on the battlefield increasingly untenable. With the development of gunpowder came numerous experiments with various types of weapons, with their size, and with the materials used in their construction. The types of projectiles used also were very varied and included darts, pellets, balls of metal or stone, and bolts with iron feathers. At this stage there were no recognized calibers, and there were many different names for the weapons. Jim Bradbury notes: "That there were various types and sizes is clear, but it is not always easy, or possible, to distinguish the contemporary meaning of the many terms used, such as cannons, bombards, culverins, veuglaires, serpentines, crapaudins, mortars, haquebuts, arquebuses, falcons, ribaudequins, guns."

Conventional wisdom has it that gunpowder was invented in China, although its use in firearms seems to have begun more or less simultaneously in the East and the West (the Chinese originally using it in fireworks). In a letter of 1249 Roger Bacon describes a recipe he arrived at after extensive experimentation and that consists of seven parts of saltpeter, five of charcoal, and five of sulfur. This was, of course, far from the only recipe: the *Liber Igneum* of Marcus Graecus from the mid-thirteenth century contained no fewer than thirty-five recipes for gunpowder. The Spanish maintained that the Moors invented it; and it also has been suggested that the Mongols used it in Japan in the thirteenth century. It is possible, therefore, that gunpowder was invented in the Far East and then taken to the West by the Muslims.

According to Bradbury:

It used to be thought that gunpowder was invented by a German monk, Berthold Schwarz of Freiburg, in the early fourteenth century. The "evidence," in the *Ghent Memorial Book,* is a later addition, and now discredited; the legend about the German monk first appeared in 1493, and was only added to the *Ghent Book* in the sixteenth century. Roger Bacon's claims, however, remain good; his work is as early as anything clearly demonstrated from elsewhere, and could well have been done independently. One point of interest is the difference between eastern and western methods of making gunpowder, at least by the sixteenth century. Balbi noted at Malta, that you could tell a Turkish shot, because the Christian smoke was "different from theirs," with its thick, black smoke.

It is far from certain how guns were invented, and by whom. It is clear enough that they appeared in Europe in the early fourteenth century, as a result of experimentation with earlier hurling engines combined with Greek fire. Bradbury informs us that the earliest representation of a cannon in the West is in the Milemete Manuscript of 1326, presented to Edward III on his accession. The weapon portrayed is shaped like a vase, apparently of metal construction, and resting horizontally on a trestle. It is firing what looks like a large crossbow bolt.

Early experiments with handheld guns produced small weapons capable of firing stones and other small projectiles. It was not long, however, before their size and range increased. At the siege of Ghent, for instance, there were no fewer than two hundred wagons containing cannons and artillery, including weapons known as ribaulds, which were mounted on large wheelbarrows.

The construction of early cannons was a complex affair. A number of rods of wrought iron were fitted around a central core, and then white-hot rings were fitted around the rods, so that when they cooled and contracted, they bound the rods together extremely tightly. Occasionally the construction would be made even more sturdy by pouring molten lead between the joints. When the whole thing had cooled, the core was removed to leave a hollow tube, into one end of which was fitted a solid chamber. Eventually wrought iron was replaced by cast iron in the construction.

At first cannons were tied to wooden platforms, which could be raised or lowered by wedges, thus altering their range. Since these platforms were often damaged by recoil, cannons were often simply placed on slopes or on purpose-built mounds of earth. On the loading of cannons, Bradbury has this to say:

> Cannons could be loaded, either by a mobile chamber or thunder-box, or at the breech. The chamber was filled with powder, leaving a tube for the heated touch. The chamber was closed with a bung of soft wood, such as alder or willow, which would not explode, but would act as a wad between the charge and the ball. The bung would expand and pop out like a champagne cork, and

this would prevent the chamber itself from exploding. A chamber consisted of a plug, and empty space for safety reasons, and three sections for powder. The mobile chamber was lifted into the breech by handles, with an iron rod to clamp it in, and was packed with tow. Mobile chambers in the lower end of the tube do not seem to have worked very well, perhaps because the clamping could not be firm enough, allowing premature ignition and a dangerous blow-out. In 1397 at Bologna one hears of a wedge being used to hold the chamber; while by the end of the fifteenth century, plugs were placed by direct loading, using rods to ram down the muzzle.

It is hardly surprising that there were many accidents with early cannons, either through exploding barrels, or chamber wedges shooting out on firing. James II of Scotland, for instance, was killed at the siege of Roxburgh in 1460 when the chamber of a bombard exploded. Such casualties were only to be expected, and with experience came improvements and refinements to weapons technology, including gunpowder. From about 1420 it became common practice to use what was known as "corned" gunpowder, which was dampened with wine (or occasionally the urine of one who drank wine), rolled into granules, and then dried. This improved the potency of the powder, as well as making it more stable.

The mid-fifteenth century saw a fashion for constructing truly gigantic cannons, such as Mons Meg, which was made for Philip of Burgundy and is now kept at Edinburgh Castle. This monster is constructed of two-and-a-half-inch-thick iron bars welded together, with iron rings welded over them to form the outer casing. It has a caliber of twenty inches, is more than thirteen feet long, and weighs five tons. Very large guns had their disadvantages, however, for although they could provide a much-needed boost to the morale of a besieging force (and, of course, have the opposite effect on the besieged), they did require a much greater amount of gunpowder, and exploded accidentally more frequently.

By the fifteenth century the cannon had become the siege engine of choice, since they were far more able to shatter walls than the mangonels of earlier times. This had the effect of making sieges much shorter-lived affairs. Henry V was brilliant both as a besieger and as a user of artillery. To the siege of Harfleur, France, during the Hundred Years' War he took sixty-five gunners, ten thousand gunstones, and some of the largest cannons then in existence. Apart from the ones he already possessed, Henry had more bombards made in London and Bristol, in addition to special mountings for the weapons that featured openings through which the target could be viewed and selected.

Usually, demand for guns concentrated on the smaller rather than the larger (monsters such as Mons Meg; Mad Margot, which weighed ten tons; and one made in 1476 and inscribed "I am the Dragon" were the exceptions rather than the rule). By the end of the medieval period they were as essential to warfare as the mounted knight had been at its height. It was through the use of cannons, for instance, that the Ottoman sultan Mehmet II was able to overwhelm the Christians at Constantinpole and take the city. Mehmet's cannons were made by a Hungarian cannon founder named Urban, who jumped at the chance to work for an employer for whom money and materials were not issues.

Urban produced some truly colossal weapons: one required fifty oxen and two thousand men to move it, and when it was tested, a warning was first sounded to prevent any pregnant women from aborting. Its stone projectiles landed a mile away, and buried themselves six feet in the ground. When deployed at Constantinople, the cannon fired balls weighing twelve hundred pounds, which made not only the walls of the city shake but also the ground inside.

The Turks also had an advantage over the Christians in the

way they maintained their weapons. The Christians within the city had to allow their cannons to cool off before firing again, and they were amazed and demoralized by how quickly their enemies could keep firing their own weapons. The Turks covered their cannons with felt, which prevented air from entering the pores in the metal and cracking it on firing; they also cooled them by soaking them in oil.

With these advances in weaponry, the role of the mounted knight became less and less significant on the battlefields of Europe and, ultimately, the rest of the world. As the centuries progressed, their function became characterized more by ritual and tradition than battle, as regular armies took their place. And yet even today, their deeds, often heroic, often terrible, live on in our imaginations, amid the spectral sounds of pounding hooves and clashing swords.

Glossary

abbot The head of an abbey or monastic community.

alchemy Strictly, the occult science of converting base metals to gold or silver; broadly, the science of medieval chemistry.

allure The wall walk behind the battlements of a castle or other fortification.

annates Taxes paid by clergy to the pope, including the first year's income from a benefice.

antichrist An enemy of Christ, expected to appear shortly before the end of the world; the word was sometimes applied to heretics.

antipope A person illegally assuming the title of pope, especially during the Great Schism of 1378–1415.

armiger A person entitled to display a coat of arms.

ashlar Stone blocks used for facing a building.

bachelor A knight who fought under another's banner.

bailey The enclosure around a castle.

ballista An engine used to propel stones and other missiles.

banneret A knight entitled to display his own banner and to lead his own retainers.

barbican A defensive addition to the main gate of a castle.

baron   The lowest-ranking hereditary peer.

bar sinister   A bar on the left of a shield, often signifying the illegitimacy of the wearer.

bastion   A defensive projection, usually in the form of a circular tower.

belfry   A siege tower.

benefice   A piece of land given to a knight by a liege lord in return for his military service.

bombard   An early form of cannon.

brattice   A wooden platform added to the battlements of a castle, with openings in the floors to enable defenders to fire or drop objects upon soldiers attacking immediately below.

bull   The seal attached to a papal or royal letter, the name later being applied to the letter itself.

burh   A primitive fortification that consisted of a refuge warriors could use in times of emergency, and which was composed of a timber palisade and a deep ditch.

cadi   A Moorish magistrate.

casemate   A gallery around the base of a castle from which defenders could fire directly into soldiers using battering rams.

catapult   A siege engine, a very large version of the modern hand-held catapult, which fired large darts.

chausses   Protective mail covering the legs.

chevauchée   A fast raid on horseback.

cluniacs   Members of a monastic order named after its motherhouse at Cluny.

constable   The principal officer in the household of a king or noble, or the governor of a royal castle.

crenellations   The battlements at the top of castle walls. The stone part was known as the merlon, and the space was called the embrasure.

curtain   The wall surrounding the bailey of a castle.

donjon   Originally the tower of a castle.

escutcheon   A shield with armorial bearings.

excommunication A punishment imposed by the church, involving exclusion from religious rites.

feudalism A modern term used to describe the medieval societies of western Europe. Government based on performance of services (including military service) in return for grants of land. Defining the term precisely with regard to medieval society is extremely difficult, and some historians argue that it should be abandoned.

fief An estate held by homage and service to a liege lord. Fiefs could vary in size from a relatively small piece of land to an entire country.

garderobe A latrine.

hauberk A coat of chain mail.

heresy A doctrine or opinions held in contradiction to established church doctrine. The penalty was usually being burned alive.

hide An area of land of approximately 120 acres.

homage A ceremony by which a tenant acknowledged his feudal allegiance to his lord.

hundred An Anglo-Saxon term for an area of land equal to 100 hides.

joust Combat between two mounted knights armed with lances.

keep The main tower of a castle.

knight service The military service owed by a knight to his liege lord.

mangonel A siege engine used to propel stones.

scutage Money paid by a feudal landowner in place of the personal and military services owed to a liege lord.

serf A tenant who was not free. The serf was legally attached to the land on which he worked. If the land was transferred to a new owner, so was the serf.

solar A private room separated from the main hall of a castle.

tournament A series of mock battles fought between two teams of knights, usually with blunted weapons, including lances that were designed to break on contact.

trebuchet   A siege engine.

trial by ordeal   A form of trial based on the assumption that God would interfere on the side of the just. One method was to throw the accused into deep water. Anyone who sank right away (and thus frequently drowned) was considered innocent. Peter Bartholomew opted for a trial by fire, with equally disastrous consequences (see chapter five).

vassal   A person holding land by feudal tenure.

virgate   Thirty acres.

Bibliography and Suggested Further Reading

In the absence of numbered footnotes I would like to acknowledge several of the works consulted in the preparation of this book that were especially helpful to me. Sir Steven Runciman's *A History of the Crusades* is, of course, the first port of call for those wishing to familiarize themselves with the period; and it has been indispensable to me in describing the life and adventures of Godfrey of Bouillon, especially with regard to the horrific events surrounding the fall of Jerusalem. Likewise, Tim Severin's marvelous travelogue of his own journey to Jerusalem in Godfrey's footsteps is incredibly evocative in its descriptions of the sights that would have greeted the Crusaders' eyes all those centuries ago, and offers many details regarding Godfrey's early life. With regard to the subjects of castles and sieges, Jim Bradbury's *The Medieval Siege* contains an enormous amount of information on the tactics employed, written in an accessible and often wryly humorous style, while Philip Warner's *The Medieval Castle* is an engaging examination of the design and construction of those magnificent buildings and of life within them. In writing the chapter on the great military orders I found Desmond Seward's masterful *The Monks of War* indispensable.

There is also a great deal of useful information available on the Internet. Among the Web sites I found most helpful are the New Advent Catholic Encyclopedia and Encyclopedia.com. The Weapons and Armour Web site furnished some essential details regarding design and construction of the knights' equipment, while the Knighthood, Chivalry, and Tournaments Resource Library provided a huge amount of useful and fascinating material on all aspects of the subject.

Books

Ayton, Andrew. *Knights and Warhorses*. Woodbridge, Eng.: The Boydell Press, 1999.

Baigent, Michael, Richard Leigh, and Henry Lincoln. *The Holy Blood and the Holy Grail*. London: Arrow Books, 1996.

Bradbury, Jim. *The Medieval Siege*. Woodbridge, Eng.: The Boydell Press, 1992.

Comnena, Anna. *The Alexiad*. London: Penguin Books, 1969.

Daraul, Arkon. *A History of Secret Societies*. New York: Citadel Press, 1994.

Froissart, Jean. *Chronicles*. Edited by John Jolliffe. London: Penguin Books, 2001.

Keen, Maurice. *The Penguin History of Medieval Europe*. London: Penguin Books, 1968.

Keen, Maurice, ed. *Medieval Warfare: A History*. Oxford: Oxford University Press, 1999.

Procacci, Giuliano. *History of the Italian People*. London: Penguin Books, 1991.

Read, Piers Paul. *The Templars*. London: Phoenix Press, 2001.

Runciman, Steven. *A History of the Crusades*. Vol. 1, *The First Crusade and the Foundation of the Kingdom of Jerusalem*. Cambridge, Eng.: Cambridge University Press, 1951.

———. *A History of the Crusades*. Vol. 2, *The Kingdom of Je-*

rusalem and the Frankish East 1100–1187. Cambridge, Eng.: Cambridge University Press, 1952.

————. *A History of the Crusades.* Vol. 3, *The Kingdom of Acre and the Later Crusades.* Cambridge, Eng.: Cambridge University Press, 1954.

Severin, Tim. *Crusader: By Horse to Jerusalem.* London: Phoenix Press, 2001.

Seward, Desmond. *The Monks of War: The Military Religious Orders.* London: Penguin Books, 1995.

Turnbull, Stephen. *The Book of the Medieval Knight.* London: Arms and Armour Press, 1995.

Warner, Philip. *The Medieval Castle: Life in a Fortress in Peace and War.* London: Penguin Books, 2001.

Web Sites

About.com
http://historymedren.about.com/

Encyclopedia.com
http://www.encyclopedia.com/

The Knighthood, Chivalry, and Tournaments Resource Library
http://www.chronique.com/

The Medieval Sourcebook
http://www.fordham.edu/halsall/sbook.html

Medieval Warfare Homepage
http://www.hyw.com/Books/History/Medi0000.htm

New Advent Catholic Encyclopedia
http://newadvent.org/cathen/

Weapons and Armour
http://members.aol.com/dargolyt/TheForge/
ALFAMAIN.HTM

Index

Index